EXPLORING
MARITIME
WASHINGTON

EXPLORING
MARITIME
WASHINGTON

A HISTORY AND GUIDE

ERICH R. EBEL

WITH CHUCK FOWLER

THE
History
PRESS

Published by The History Press
Charleston, SC
www.historypress.com

First published 2023

Manufactured in the United States

ISBN 9781467150576

Library of Congress Control Number: 2022949583

To Walter Ebel, my father, who instilled in me a love for the history, heritage and culture of Washington, its Indigenous peoples and its waterways by taking me places to experience them instead of simply learning about them from books or stories. From our first boating class to our myriad fishing trips, Native salmon bakes and historical hikes around the coast, through you I learned to cherish the places that so many of us call home. Thank you.

CONTENTS

FOREWORD

I was raised on the western shore of Bainbridge Island in Puget Sound at a little place called Crystal Springs. Because we had a dock and a float, many boats of all shapes, sizes and purposes stopped at our dock. Each one of them fascinated me from childhood. Over the years, I have watched our maritime history change and much of it, unfortunately, disappear. Thankfully, in 2019, after decades of advocacy and effort by state maritime history groups, historians, museums, educators, Indigenous tribes, elected officials and many others, Congress created the Maritime Washington National Heritage Area (MWNHA). A major impetus for its establishment was the 1989 Washington state centennial commemoration. I was honored to co-chair the one hundredth anniversary event alongside the state's first lady, Jean Gardner. Among its many history-themed projects, those based on Washington's diverse maritime heritage were some of the most memorable. Careful planning, diligence and hard work in the years that followed led to the creation of the first strictly maritime-themed National Heritage Area in the nation.

Between November 1988 and November 1989, almost two hundred individual maritime activities and events took place throughout the state. Two of the milestone projects that highlighted Washington's cross-cultural maritime roots were the Paddle to Seattle—a journey of traditionally designed Native Salish cedar canoes and paddlers from Suquamish tribal lands across Puget Sound to a landing and welcoming in Seattle—and the construction, launch and first voyage of the eighteenth-century square-rigged replica sailing ship *Lady Washington*. Both projects symbolized and signaled a new awareness of the importance of relationships between the state's original inhabitants and the Euro-Americans who arrived beginning in the late eighteenth century. More importantly, they offered the opportunity to reconcile sometimes contentious, confrontational early encounters between Indigenous residents and the newly arrived explorers and settlers.

The Paddle to Seattle became the major Native-developed cultural and maritime heritage event of the centennial year. Incredible pictures of the canoe fleet crossing Puget Sound appeared in local and national news publications with Seattle in the background, soon reaching a worldwide audience. This event spawned the ongoing Tribal Canoe Journeys program, a successful Native cultural education and youth development program involving hundreds of Native-designed canoes gathering at various tribal communities throughout coastal Washington and the MWNHA.

The construction of the *Lady Washington* was part of an effort to recreate the first two American sailing ships to visit the Pacific Northwest. In 1788, the *Lady Washington*—commanded by Captain Robert Gray—arrived first, followed by the larger *Columbia Rediviva*. These two ships, backed by Boston merchants, established the first American presence on the northwest coast, as well as in Hawaii to develop the newly expanding Pan-Pacific fur trade business.

In the decades since its launch, the *Lady* has been Washington's tall ship ambassador and floating educational classroom, visiting communities throughout Puget Sound, along Washington's coast and up the Columbia River. The *Lady* has logged thousands of miles and welcomed more than one million visitors across its decks since its launch, including a quarter-million students who've participated in her hands-on shipboard education programs.

The annual Tribal Canoe Journeys and the construction and operation of the *Lady Washington* are successful, unique, foundational elements of the MWNHA, offering residents and visitors alike extraordinary opportunities to experience the state's rich maritime history and contribute to greater understanding of our deep cross-cultural heritage.

I hope that *Exploring Maritime Washington* will allow you to travel the state's highways, byways and waterways and discover the hundreds of fascinating stories and experiences along Washington's unique historical coastline.

Ralph Munro
Washington Secretary of State, 1981–2001

ACKNOWLEDGEMENTS

I t would be impossible to fit the entirety of Washington's maritime history into a book of this size. There are far too many fascinating stories, culturally significant destinations and critical background points to tell the complete nautical narrative of this great state. With each successive interview of a local historical expert or visit to a harbor or coastal community, it became apparent that I would have to winnow the topics to focus on the *truly* unique or the *most hidden* gems. Even that presented challenges, as I felt compelled to honor the passions of each dedicated museum volunteer, historical society board member, tribal cultural resource officer and destination marketing representative who permitted me an interview or assisted with research. Ultimately, I included as much of the best material as I could—but in no way does it represent the totality of the always fascinating, sometimes terrifying, often inspiring and even humorous history that comprises the raw material with which the community of Washington was built. This book represents the shared maritime history of so many people who deserve adulation for their own research, collections and dedication to preservation.

I'd like to begin by acknowledging the members of Washington's tribes (both federally recognized and non–federally recognized) who assisted with the creation of this book. Those include members of the Chinook Nation, Cowlitz Tribe, Duwamish Tribe, Hoh Tribe, Jamestown S'Klallam Tribe,

Lower Elwha Klallam Tribe, Lummi Nation, Makah Tribe, Nisqually Tribe, Port Gamble S'Klallam Tribe, Puyallup Tribe, Quileute Nation, Quinault Nation, Samish Nation, Shoalwater Bay Tribe, Skokomish Tribe, Squaxin Island Tribe, Steilacoom Tribe, Suquamish Tribe, Swinomish Tribe and Tulalip Tribes.

Additionally, there are several historical societies, museums and heritage organizations that deserve credit for making this book possible. Those include the Friends of Lime Kiln Society, San Juan Historical Society and Museum, Lopez Island Historical Society and Museum, Museum of the North Beach, International Mermaid Museum, Westport South Beach Historical Society and Maritime Museum, Willapa Seaport Museum, Knappton Cove Heritage Center, Lewis and Clark Trail Heritage Foundation, The Historic Trust, Two Rivers Heritage Museum, Poulsbo Historical Society and Maritime Museum, Cowlitz County Historical Society and Museum, Working Waterfront Coalition of Whatcom County, Harbor History Museum, Sequim Museum and Arts, Mason County Historical Society Museum, Point Roberts Historical Society, Washington State Archives, Lighthouse Friends and, of course, all the stewards of Washington historical knowledge at HistoryLink.org.

Further, many of the breathtaking photos and location recommendations included in this book are courtesy of the myriad destination marketing organizations, visitor and convention bureaus and tourism alliances that help promote all facets of life in Washington. Those include the San Juan Islands Visitors Bureau, Visit Vancouver USA, Olympic Peninsula Visitor Bureau, Whidbey and Camano Islands Tourism and Bellingham Whatcom County Tourism.

The impetus for this book's creation is Congress's designation of the Maritime Washington National Heritage Area (MWNHA), which is managed by the Washington Trust for Historic Preservation. Along with several individuals, organizations and agencies—including my author colleague, Chuck Fowler—the Trust has been striving toward that goal for well over three decades. I'd like to acknowledge the hard work and effort of Chris Moore and Alex Gradwohl with the Washington Trust, members of the MWNHA steering committee, the state Department of Archaeology and Historic Preservation, contributors to the 2011 National Maritime Heritage Area feasibility study, contributors to the 2011 Maritime Resource Survey for Washington's Saltwater Shores and everyone in Washington who has worked to make this a reality.

Finally, where would I be without the support and endless patience of my family? All my love and gratitude for enduring the late nights and long hours go deservedly to you. Thank you.

WASHINGTON'S MARITIME HISTORY

AN INTRODUCTION

When one thinks of the maritime history of the United States, the focus naturally is on its chronological beginnings on the Atlantic coast. History books frequently detail the romanticized (and some say mischaracterized) "discovery of America" by Italian explorer Christopher Columbus aboard the ships *Niña*, *Pinta* and *Santa Maria* in 1492; the landing of the first permanent English settlers aboard the *Susan Constant*, *Godspeed* and *Discovery* in Jamestown, Virginia, in 1607; and the subsequent arrival of persecuted Pilgrims from England on the *Mayflower* in Massachusetts in 1620. Today, these well-known early milestones and sites of maritime history are also widely chronicled, commemorated and visited by thousands at the popular shoreside sites that, in many cases, feature replicas of the vessels that carried early European explorers and settlers to the East Coast.

While the early land settlement of the Atlantic coast was underway in the late fifteenth and early sixteeth centuries, nearly three thousand miles away on the Pacific coast, both British and Spanish seagoing explorers were also probing the lands north of Mexico in California and farther up the continent. In the 1570s, English captain Sir Francis Drake sailed his ship *Golden Hind* to present-day Oregon but did not lay national claim to the land. However, later, in the 1770s, Captain Juan Pérez entered the territory and claimed what is now British Columbia for Spain. The Russians also made limited forays into what is now Alaska but did not venture farther south. During this two-century-long period, settlement and commercial expansion—mainly based on the fur trade—developed slowly on the Pacific coast.

It wasn't until the late eighteenth century, in 1792, shortly after the American Revolution erupted on the Atlantic coast, that British and American maritime expansion took off in the Pacific Northwest. The British government sent navy captain George Vancouver to explore the shores of present-day western Canada in search of a hoped-for Northwest Passage linking the eastern and western sides of the North American continent. From aboard two ships, *Discovery* and *Chatham*, and their longboats, Vancouver took extensive scientific sightings and soundings and named hundreds of geographical locations, including the extensive inland sea, Puget Sound, which he named for his lieutenant Peter Puget. At the same time and in the same location, American captain Robert Gray, aboard his ships *Columbia Rediviva* and *Lady Washington*, had been dispatched by Boston merchants in search of sites to secure profitable otter furs as a commercial enterprise, rather than mapping and naming territory.

When Vancouver first observed what would become Washington, he wrote in his expedition journal about his travels past a vast forest broken by pleasant meadows reminiscent of the English countryside and backed by towering mountains. Vancouver and other crew members chronicled their interactions with the original residents of the region, the Indigenous Coast Salish people who had occupied and cared for the region's environment and resources for at least 12,500 years—or as their cultural and spiritual leaders refer to it, "since time immemorial."

Geologically, Washington developed over many millions of years before initial habitation by humans and subsequent sightings by European American explorers and entrepreneurs. Archaeologists have concluded that the area's first known human Indigenous residents, the Coast Salish people, arrived at least 12,500 years ago. This makes Puget Sound one of the longest continuously inhabited landscapes in the continental United States. People came to this area to take advantage of the abundant resources, including salmon, vast tracts of forests and a wide variety of rock types that could be hewn into exquisite stone tools, including adzes and knives to carve cedar canoes.

After settlement and population growth on the Atlantic Seaboard began approaching what felt like critical mass in the late 1700s, President Thomas Jefferson kicked off the nineteenth century by dispatching Captain Meriwether Lewis and Lieutenant William Clark to lead the Corps of Discovery Expedition in 1804. Their mission was simple, yet unimaginably difficult in execution: explore the lands west of the Mississippi River that comprised the Louisiana Purchase. Along the way, they confronted challenges such as unforgiving terrain, harsh weather, treacherous waters, starvation, injuries, disease and both friendly and hostile Native Americans. Nevertheless, the journey was a success in that they reached the Pacific Ocean in what is now Washington and provided America with new geographic, ecological and cultural information about previously uncharted areas of the continent.

Within decades, the British Hudson's Bay Company (HBC) began siting trading posts on the Pacific coast to take advantage of the rich supply of beaver, otter and other furs that were lucrative in the early 1800s. This had an added benefit of establishing a British presence on these so-called unoccupied lands, thereby reinforcing territorial claims made for the Crown. As the United States grew into a fledgling country, it, too, wanted to expand its realm and sent American lieutenant Charles Wilkes and the U.S. Exploring Expedition on a mission to sail to the Pacific and explore its farthest reaches, including the Pacific Northwest, which he did from 1838 through 1842. Many of the places and geographical features in Washington today were either named by Vancouver or Gray or renamed by Wilkes.

Shortly after Wilkes mapped the waterways of Puget Sound, the specter of Manifest Destiny overtook many Americans living in the East and Midwest. By the late 1840s, thousands of emigrants were packing up their families and possessions into wagons and heading across a mostly unknown and dangerous overland route that became the Oregon Trail. It was shortly after this push to the West that Washington became a territory of its own and needed a governor to help forge its destiny.

President Franklin Pierce named his comrade-in-arms and political supporter General Isaac Stevens to be the first governor of the new territory and tasked him almost immediately with surveying a route for a transcontinental railroad, maintaining order and persuading the area's Indigenous population to make room for the influx of pioneer settlers from the East. Stevens undertook a whirlwind tour of the territory, convincing Natives who barely understood what was taking place to sign unfair treaties relinquishing their traditional lands and agreeing to relocate to tiny reservations chosen by the American government. While these treaties ensured certain rights would remain with the Indians, the government often failed to live up to its side of the bargain, leading ultimately to an ongoing period of revolt known as the Treaty Wars in the mid-1850s.

Once the uprising had been put down with the help of the U.S. Army and scores of volunteer companies mustered from among the ranks of settlers, Americans set about developing their industrial and maritime interests in the new lands. Sawmills, fish canneries, mining operations and shipping ports sprang up across the area, bringing fame and fortune to some—and heartbreak and misery to others. For displaced Native peoples watching their culture nearly eradicated by conquest and imported diseases, the latter was always the case.

In the mid-twentieth century, however, something monumental happened. Washington's tribes united behind a common cultural cause and, from that, began experiencing a reinvigoration of their heritage. A Nisqually Indian leader named Billy Frank Jr. rallied others to fight for the fishing rights that were guaranteed them by the treaties signed a century earlier. In 1974, a federal judge named George Boldt decided a landmark lawsuit in favor of the tribes, thereby upholding their fishing rights and ensuring their rightful place in Washington's future.

For the past two centuries, the maritime history of Washington, both its positive and negative aspects, has been largely told separately in Native and European American contexts. But three decades ago, during the Washington state centennial commemoration in 1989, a new, more culturally diverse and unified heritage approach developed. It respected Native and immigrant cultures, acknowledged and expressed remorse for past transgressions and told a more authentic, integrated story of the development of the state and its people.

More recently, in early 2019, this movement was permanently commemorated when Congress established the new Maritime Washington National Heritage Area (MWNHA), thus allowing the unique history, features and stories of the north Pacific coast of the United States to receive long-overdue attention. Managed by the National Park Service, the MWNHA is the result of a comprehensive, yearslong study process conducted by the designated coordinating organization, the Washington Trust for Historic Preservation. It included an extensive outreach program that involved hundreds of maritime heritage and education organizations as well as individuals that included the region's original residents, the Indigenous people and tribes.

This historical travel guidebook seeks to provide Washington residents as well as visitors from near and far a more comprehensive, inclusive picture and understanding of the maritime heritage of Washington. The uniqueness of *Exploring Maritime Washington* is based on providing the history enthusiast and traveler a hands-on guide to the state's myriad cross-cultural attractions, sites and stories. By visiting and experiencing Washington's special maritime features—museums, ships, lighthouses, waterfronts and all—the heritage traveler can obtain an authentic understanding of maritime Washington's diverse, inclusive history and culture.

The guide is divided into five sections—Central Puget Sound, North Puget Sound, South Puget Sound, the Olympic Peninsula and the Columbia River. While the MWNHA covers nearly three thousand miles of Washington's coastline, it doesn't fully extend deep into the Columbia River, where tidal activity is still noticeable. This book does, and each section contains hub cities from which maritime explorers may choose to venture out to other destinations.

This historical guidebook, prepared by lifelong residents who are also knowledgeable historians and seasoned travelers, offers insider information, hidden gems and special stories that make Washington's maritime history truly extraordinary. We hope you enjoy using it to explore and discover maritime Washington.

Chuck Fowler

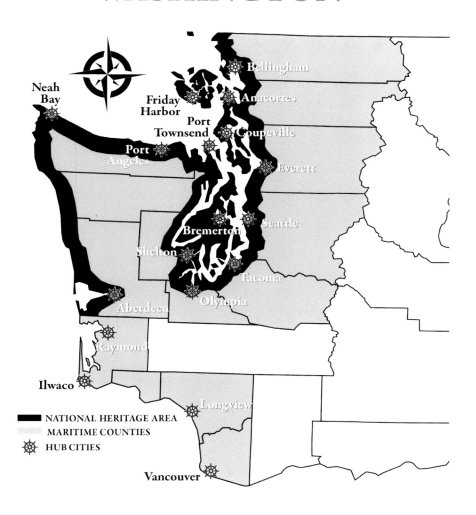

WESTERN
WASHINGTON

Neah
Bay

Friday
Harbor

Bellingham

Anacortes

Port
Townsend

Coupeville

Port
Angeles

Everett

Bremerton

Seattle

Shelton

Tacoma

Aberdeen

Olympia

Raymond

Ilwaco

Longview

Vancouver

NATIONAL HERITAGE AREA
MARITIME COUNTIES
HUB CITIES

PART I

CENTRAL
PUGET SOUND

King, Snohomish
and Kitsap Counties

HUB CITY: SEATTLE

There is so much maritime history in Washington's largest and most populated city, it could be tempting to limit how far a visitor is willing to explore. However, given the sheer number of fascinating attractions within a day's short drive, it would be a mistake not to venture a bit farther to see what lies just down the road.

Seattle was, at one time, just another tiny settlement struggling for permanence. The city is named after siʔałˀ, a pivotal leader among the Indigenous Duwamish and Suquamish peoples. However, it was also known as New York, New York Alki (a Chinook Jargon word that translates to "by and by") and Duwamps to settlers in the mid-1800s.

When the first non-Native people landed in what is now West Seattle in November 1851, they brought with them just over twenty men, women and children from the Willamette Valley near present-day Portland, Oregon. Though not the first white people to set foot in the area, they were the first permanent non-Indian residents. Today, a historical marker along Alki Avenue SW at the northern end of Sixty-Third Avenue SW denotes the approximate landing site. By late 1852, more settlers began calling the small community home—including Dr. David Maynard, who convinced his new neighbors to name the settlement after Seattle, and Henry Yesler, an industrialist who built the area's first steam-powered sawmill.

Seattle has endured its share of difficulties throughout history. In 1856, the so-called Battle of Seattle pitted a handful of local tribal warriors against a barrage of artillery from the U.S. Navy sloop *Decatur* during the Treaty

Wars. The twelve-hour conflict was fairly inconsequential, but it frightened many of Seattle's early residents into permanently relocating. By the time the lumber mills had backfilled their workforce and resumed activity, they were joined by new mining and fishing businesses that also depended on sea transportation.

Labor riots and racial intolerance in the 1880s led to economic depression in the early 1890s, which faded quickly with the Klondike Gold Rush of 1897. Seattle reinvented itself as the "Gateway to Alaska," as tens of thousands of gold-hungry prospectors flooded into the city en route to the Yukon gold fields. Entrepreneurs capitalized by selling supplies and services to miners waiting for ships heading north, and soon Seattle's population swelled from about forty-two thousand in 1890 to nearly half a million people by 1910. Even the Great Seattle Fire of 1899, which leveled over one hundred acres of the city's business district, did not seem to dissuade residents from evolving their growing community.

Through its bust periods and its boom periods, Seattle has always weathered the storms of time by relying on its maritime resources. In the earliest days, when mining, fishing and timber dominated the economy, those commodities had to be shipped to be profitable, which employed a small army of dockworkers, boat captains and crew. Seattle has also had a steady stream of seafood-related industries, whether catching, processing, canning or distributing the product. These early commercial activities grew the Port of Seattle from its creation in 1913 into the fifth-busiest cargo-moving operation in the country, seeing tens of billions of dollars in commodities imported and exported annually.

The need to traverse western Washington's unique waterways gave rise to a fleet of transportation vessels so active that they looked to some like a swarm of mosquitoes on the Puget Sound—hence the nickname "the Mosquito Fleet." During wartime, Seattle's shipbuilding industry, led by Robert Moran and the Moran Brothers Shipyard, rivaled that of other major American port cities like Baltimore and San Francisco. And recently, Seattle has become a travel destination for international cruise ships filled with visitors looking to experience the natural beauty and salty wonder of the Pacific Northwest.

Lighthouse enthusiasts will appreciate the impressive selection of historic beacons, such as the West Point Lighthouse (1881), the Alki Point Lighthouse (1913) and the Point Robinson Lighthouse on nearby Maury Island (1884). Seattle also boasts an active U.S. Coast Guard base, which includes the Coast Guard Museum Northwest, home to an impressive collection of lighthouse memorabilia, nautical items, ship models, historical photographs and the area's largest public collection of Coast Guard patches. Visitors can request a free pass from the sentry at the gate and find the museum on base at Pier 36, 1519 South Alaskan Way.

MUSEUM OF HISTORY AND INDUSTRY

One of the first stops a maritime visitor to Seattle should make is at the Museum of History and Industry (known locally as MOHAI and pronounced "MOW-high"), 860 North Terry Avenue at the south end of Lake Union. Set in the historic Naval Reserve Building that once housed thousands of sailors training for World War II, the remodeled structure is now home to a modern museum dedicated to collecting and preserving artifacts and stories of the Puget Sound region's diverse history. In addition

Located in the heart of downtown Seattle, South Lake Union Park is the maritime heritage hub of Puget Sound. It is the home of the Museum of History and Industry (MOHAI), Northwest Seaport and its fleet of historic ships (*lower right*) and the Center for Wooden Boats (*lower left*). *Brian Morris.*

to absorbing a thorough education on Seattle's storied past, visitors can also take in exhibits and programs that highlight the city's present conditions and offer insight into its future.

Visitors to MOHAI can tour dozens of exhibits to get the complete perspective of Seattle's maritime and historical evolution, from its Indigenous cultures through the founding of Amazon and Microsoft. One of the most visually impressive maritime exhibits greets patrons in the main hall: an unmissable eleven-thousand-pound, sixty-four-foot-high sculpture named *Wawona*, after a historic 1897 schooner that holds a special place in the city's heart. The sculpture is made of over two hundred wood panels salvaged from the ship before it was scrapped in 2009 and is meant to conjure the image of a sailing ship's hull while invoking the impression of an old-growth tree.

When first launched, *Wawona* was North America's largest-ever three-masted schooner at 166 feet long with a 36-foot beam and a full crew of over thirty men. Named after a Native American word for spotted owl, *Wawona* made Washington its home port beginning in 1914 after spending nearly two decades hauling lumber up and down the Pacific coast. In the 1920s, an Anacortes company purchased the ship and refitted it for cod fishing. Plying the waters off Alaska's coast and the Bering Sea, *Wawona* could stay out for up to six months before returning with record-setting numbers of fish. According to HistoryLink.org, the ship set the all-time total catch record by a single vessel in the 1940s: 6,830,400.

During World War II, the military refitted *Wawona* to haul cargo to remote Alaskan outposts and return with lumber for the aviation industry, but by the time the war ended, technology had outpaced the ship's usefulness. The schooner, old but not yet historical, sat unused and deteriorating for decades. In the 1960s, a dedicated group of citizens (that later became the Northwest Seaport organization) purchased the ship, intending to convert it into a maritime museum—a noble but complicated pursuit. For another twenty years, *Wawona* languished in port as supporters tried in vain to raise enough to restore it to a manageable condition. During that time, the ship became a National Historic Site as well as an official Seattle landmark; however, nothing could stop the relentless march of time.

In 2009, despite every last-minute attempt to rescue the aging vessel, *Wawona* was finally dismantled. Local artist John Grade salvaged parts of the ship to create the nearly five-story lobby sculpture greeting visitors to MOHAI, which is all that remains of the once-proud vestige of Washington's timber and fishing heritage.

Once part of the Northwest Seaport heritage fleet, the schooner *Wawona* is shown here carrying a full load of lumber down the Pacific coast to California in 1899. *Northwest Seaport.*

Following the sculpture from ground to ceiling will surprise visitors with a hidden gem awaiting them on the top floor at MOHAI. The Puget Sound Maritime Historical Society maintains a permanent exhibit there that explores the various water-related activities associated with the city, the Puget Sound and the Pacific Northwest. Patrons can peer into a World War II–era submarine periscope that extends through the roof of the building to get a 360-degree view of the South Lake Union area. Maritime enthusiasts can learn about Seattle's remarkable shipbuilding history—including the Moran Brothers Company, which built the World War I battleship USS *Nebraska*—and get an up-close view of the 1885 Fresnel lens that once guided ships through the Strait of Juan de Fuca from the long-gone Smith Island lighthouse just west of Whidbey Island. One of the most entertaining components of the maritime exhibit is a digital interactive table that immerses the participant in the role of a Mosquito Fleet ship captain in a race against another passenger vessel—a friendly competition that was quite common when steamships plied the waters of Puget Sound.

Historic Ships Wharf

Perhaps the best place to see one of the last remaining Mosquito Fleet ships is just outside MOHAI along Historic Ships Wharf at the north end of Lake Union Park, home to a half-dozen historically significant vessels. Visitors can stroll along the wharf reading about the histories of these ships and photographing them and even take a tour. In the first slip resides the steamer *Virginia V*, a National Historic Landmark. *Virginia V* (known as "Virginia Five" today, or "Virginia Vee" to the remaining few who experienced the ship in its heyday) is a century-old Mosquito Fleet steamship constructed from locally sourced old-growth fir. The fifth to carry the Virginia moniker, "Vee" began servicing the Seattle-Tacoma route in 1922, ferrying thousands of passengers across Puget Sound until 1942. For a time, *Virginia V* worked on the Columbia River shuttling passengers from Portland to Astoria, Oregon, but the ship struggled to reinvent itself in an increasingly gasoline-powered world.

By 1976, a nonprofit organization called the Steamer Virginia V Foundation formed to purchase and preserve the aging vessel and successfully raised the funds to do so. In 1995, *Virginia V* began receiving a complete overhaul, which lasted several years. In 2002, the restored and refitted *Virginia V* returned to service on the Puget Sound as a charter vessel and maritime festival participant, allowing enthusiasts to have one of the most uniquely Northwest experiences available in Washington today.

Floating right beside *Virginia V* is the tugboat *Arthur Foss*, more than thirty years older than its Mosquito Fleet neighbor. In fact, it's the oldest vessel still afloat in the Pacific Northwest. Built in 1889, the same year Washington received statehood, *Arthur Foss* is one of the founding members of a vast fleet of tugs built by the Foss Launch and Tug Company (known today as Foss Maritime). At one time, its job was to shepherd sailing vessels across the treacherous Columbia River Bar into Astoria. During the Klondike Gold Rush, *Arthur Foss* towed barges to and from the gold fields in Alaska, and in 1933, it was featured in the film *Tugboat Annie*, based loosely on the life of Tacoma businesswoman Thea Foss, the company's founder and namesake.

In 1941, *Arthur Foss* was one of the last ships to leave Wake Island before the Japanese invasion; another ship in the Foss fleet remained behind and was captured. After the war, *Arthur Foss* continued its company service until its retirement in 1968. Two years later, Foss Maritime donated the ship to Northwest Seaport, which found more success restoring the tug than it had restoring *Wawona*. *Arthur Foss* became a National Historic Landmark in 1989, its centennial year, and is currently open for tours and public enjoyment throughout the year.

Next in the lineup are two unique service vessels that each played a part in the history of western Washington—the fireboat *Duwamish*, which protected Seattle's wooden waterfront from 1909 to 1985, and Lightship No. 83 *Swiftsure*, a floating beacon to help guide maritime vessels where no lighthouses could be built. For ninety-four years, *Duwamish* was the world's most powerful fireboat, able to pump 22,800 gallons of water per minute through its nozzles. Just four years after it launched, *Duwamish* was integral in fighting the Grand Trunk Pacific dock fire on the Seattle waterfront, which leveled the structure in just two hours. The blaze resulted in dozens of injuries and several deaths, but it did not spread to the neighboring Colman dock, thanks to *Duwamish*'s efforts. *Duwamish* now serves as a museum ship to tell the story of Seattle's maritime firefighting history.

Swiftsure, one of the more unique ships to behold, is the oldest of its kind in the United States. Launched in 1904, Lightship No. 83 (as it's officially known) protected sailors up and down the Pacific coast until 1960 and still retains its original steam engine. Lightships were traditionally named after the station to which they were assigned but were given numerical identifiers in 1867 to make recordkeeping easier. *Swiftsure*'s last point of service was off the Swiftsure Bank in the Strait of Juan de Fuca between Washington and Vancouver Island, Canada. During its period of service, Lightship No. 83 was known successively as *Blunts Reef*, *San Francisco*, *Relief* and *Swiftsure*, and it helped rescue hundreds of people from dozens of stranded and sinking ships. It is currently undergoing a massive restoration, courtesy of Northwest Seaport. Both *Duwamish* and *Swiftsure* are official Seattle Landmarks as well as National Historic Landmarks.

Rounding out this historical cast of characters is the latest addition to Historic Ships Wharf. The schooner *Tordenskjold* was built in 1911 in Seattle's Ballard neighborhood. It spent over a century fishing the North Pacific for halibut, cod, tuna, crab, shrimp and more. *Tordenskjold*—affectionately called "Tordie"—retired from service in 2012 and was donated to Northwest Seaport five years later.

Visitors to Historic Ships Wharf will often find other historic ships temporarily moored there, so there's no telling what surprises may be in store when exploring South Lake Union.

The Center for Wooden Boats

Within shouting distance of MOHAI is a unique destination that no maritime enthusiast will want to miss. Located at 1010 Valley Street in Seattle, the Center for Wooden Boats (CWB) is a place where visitors can learn about the history of the boatbuilding craft, rent a variety of wooden boats to take out on Lake Union, enroll in a sailing or boating class and observe expert boatbuilders in the shop.

CWB was the brainchild of a man named Dick Wagner in the 1970s; he and his wife turned their wooden boat–rental business into a passion project that evolved into one of the Northwest's more interesting maritime heritage organizations. The main Wagner Education Center contains a small interpretive center and gift shop, a classroom space and the main boatbuilding shop. However, just a few dozen steps from the building is the CWB dock complex, where visitors can ogle privately owned floating wooden masterpieces, peruse the selection of watercraft available for rent, watch expert shipwrights make repairs, eavesdrop on an outdoor knot-tying class or just stroll the length of the dock, taking in the sights.

Thanks to the CWB's Public Peapod Program, anyone can take a wooden rowboat out on Lake Union free of charge. With a little advance notice (and an online reservation at CWB.org), vacationers can create a memorable, no-cost experience for up to five adults. Alternatively, several types of rowboats, kayaks, canoes and paddleboards are available for rent at the boathouse. For the truly adventurous, CWB offers sailing lessons, a variety of youth sailing camps and intimate charter cruises aboard either a historic fishing vessel or a romantic fantail launch.

Duwamish Longhouse and Cultural Center

One of the most uniquely fascinating aspects of Washington is the history of its Indigenous peoples, especially those with deep connections to the water. There are twenty-nine federally recognized tribes with traditional lands inside Washington's borders and a handful of non–federally recognized tribes still seeking acknowledgement by the U.S. government. Achieving federal recognition is a complex process resulting from centuries of delicately built relationships that were often sabotaged by broken promises, racist policies and even acts of indescribable violence—but the tribes and nations in Washington today are strong and thriving, having persevered through these challenges while retaining the beauty and culture of their heritage.

As with all lands in western Washington, Indigenous tribes had populated the area for millennia prior to the arrival of European Americans. The land between today's cities of Shoreline and Federal Way was full of villages, camps and longhouses belonging to the Duwamish, an anglicization of the word dxʷdəwʔabš. Known as the People of the Inside for their location on the mainland along Elliott Bay's eastern shore, the Duwamish subsisted by fishing for salmon, harvesting shellfish, gathering roots and berries and hunting animals. Many would move from place to place as the seasons changed and resources shifted, which led to the development of a vast trading network between neighboring tribes. Though their access to the water was critical to their survival, it also included the ever-present danger of attack from outsiders.

Whether traveling among villages, fishing or engaging in conflict with other tribes, the Duwamish people depended on canoes for their survival. The tribe used seven types of canoes for varying purposes. Some styles proved more stable for river travel; other styles required a sleeker design for hunting or speed. Tribal members carved wider canoes to haul supplies, whereas canoes with high bows were better suited to cut though tumultuous ocean waves. So embedded is the canoe in Duwamish culture that it was considered equal in importance to a family's home.

The Duwamish people lived and worked in this region for thousands of years before the arrival of the first non-Natives in their waters. Seattle, as a young boy, is said to have watched from shore as George Vancouver's ten-cannon survey ship, the HMS *Discovery*, first sailed into what is now Puget Sound in 1792. When the *Discovery* and the HMS *Chatham* anchored off the coast of Bainbridge Island that year, it was the Duwamish and Suquamish peoples who first welcomed the British to their homeland.

Like most of the region's tribal population, the Duwamish and Suquamish peoples saw their homes, lands and indeed traditional way of life eventually taken by the American government through treaties in the mid-1850s. In 1855, Washington territorial governor Isaac Stevens obtained the signatures of tribal headmen from the Duwamish, Suquamish and others on the Treaty of Point Elliott near what is now the town of Mukilteo. Congress ratified the document in 1859, forcing the Duwamish Tribe to hand over fifty-four thousand acres of land that today makes up the cities of Seattle, Bellevue and more. Additionally, the government refused to honor agreements establishing multiple land reservations it had negotiated with the Duwamish, which would have given them much of present-day Tukwila, Renton and the West Seattle Peninsula. Until just within the past thirty years or so, the canoe culture of the Duwamish steadily waned as Euro-American influence took its toll. However, during the celebration of Washington's statehood centennial in 1989, something happened that turned the tide for traditional Coast Salish culture.

An elder named Emmett Oliver from the Quinault Nation on the state's west coast, who served as the state's supervisor for Indian education under then-governor Booth Gardener, had been searching for a way to revive tribal traditions in the Pacific Northwest to coincide with the state's centennial activities. Oliver convinced Gardner to include eight hand-carved canoes in the ceremonies and invite First Nations tribes from Canada to participate in the festivities. Calling it the Paddle to Seattle, these tribes joined others who had heard about the movement, and on July 21, 1989, canoe after canoe came ashore at a park in north Seattle—an event that brought some tribal elders who had not witnessed such an occurrence in over half a century to tears. For days, participants took part in canoe races, cooked Indigenous foods, reunited with distant family members and forged new relationships with other tribes where none may have existed before, and the seeds of a new tradition began to take root in the hearts of the young.

Since that first momentous event held on the traditional shores of the Duwamish, American and Canadian tribes have repeated the near-annual celebration, now called Tribal Canoe Journeys, with a different tribe hosting each landing. What began as a way for Washington tribes to take part in the celebration of a statehood they never asked for has organically evolved into something that inspires pride in each subsequent generation of participants. It has become more than an event, fanning the flames of a rich heritage that was once threatened with being extinguished forever.

The Duwamish Tribe today, though still not federally recognized, maintains a remarkably beautiful Longhouse and Cultural Center to help educate guests about canoe culture and tell their story. Visitors to the center at 4705 West Marginal Way SW can learn about the social, cultural and economic survival of the Duwamish Tribe through artifacts unearthed in archaeological excavations as well as contemporary art and interpretive displays. Much like the traditional structures of long ago, today's longhouse helps keep the culture alive and thriving.

SEATTLE'S WATERFRONT AND MINER'S LANDING

Visitors to the Seattle Waterfront today can still catch hidden glimpses of its history beneath the flashy facades and modern storefronts. From the humblest of beginnings as a crude wharf attached to Henry Yesler's sawmill in 1852 to the vast, thriving international tourist destination it has become, the Seattle Waterfront has undergone a terrific transformation over a century in the making. In its early days, Yesler's sawmill at the end of Mill Street (nicknamed "Skid Road" and known today as Yesler Way) was lost to fire and rebuilt at least twice before the wharf itself finally burned in the Great Seattle Fire of 1889. By the time Yesler rebuilt his wharf, several larger, more modern structures had sprung up beside it.

Yesler's wharf evolved over time to become Pier 1 and Pier 2. Later operated by the Alaska Steamship Company, the piers were renamed to accommodate the growing commercial waterfront. The area where Piers 1 and 2 once stood became the site of Piers 50, 51 and 52, which saw a variety of uses over time. After its destruction in the Great Seattle Fire, the rebuilt Pier 52 became an iconic feature of the Seattle Waterfront. Boasting a domed passenger waiting area and a seventy-two-foot clock tower, Colman Dock (as it was known after its 1882 construction) served as the primary location for the vast Mosquito Fleet.

One spring night in 1912, the captain of the *Alameda* ordered his engineer to reverse on approaching Colman Dock. Somehow mishearing the order, the engineer accelerated instead, and the ship smashed into the dock at full speed. The clock tower collapsed into the bay, a sternwheeler moored at the dock split open and sank and the damage to the steel-hulled *Alameda* was incredible. In the aftermath, crews recovered the wreckage of the clock tower, successfully raised the sunken sternwheeler and repaired the damage to the *Alameda* and Colman Dock. Unbelievably, no one was injured in the spectacular crash.

Just north of Colman Dock, the Grand Trunk Pacific dock served as a waterfront headquarters for the company that built the second trans-Canadian railroad line. On a sweltering summer afternoon in 1914, fire broke out inside the warehouse. Two ships moored to the dock spotted the smoke and disembarked, notifying the fire department. In those days, the wooden pilings used on the waterfront were coated with creosote, a water-resistant but extremely flammable tar-like substance, which caused the fire to quickly engulf the entire building. The blaze burned so hot that a fuel tank aboard one of the responding fire engines exploded, injuring several

Many of today's active Seattle tourist attractions, restaurants and gift shops are housed in Seattle's historic working waterfront warehouses built along Elliott Bay in the early 1900s. *RonaldL.*

firefighters. One of the only positive outcomes of the inferno was that it tested Seattle's newest fireboat, the *Duwamish*, which rose admirably to the challenge. The Grand Trunk Pacific dock fire was extinguished within hours but resulted in five deaths and twenty-nine injuries. The dock was rebuilt, but the company soon went bankrupt.

During the World's Fair in 1962, the piers supported several restaurants as well as ships that functioned as floating hotels—known as "boatels." Once the event ended and the crowds dispersed, Piers 51 and 52 were demolished to make room for the fledgling Washington State Ferry system, and today, they serve as the staging area for passenger vehicles waiting to board.

No stroll along the Seattle Waterfront should be considered complete without a lunchtime visit to Ivar's, a Northwest original since 1938. Founded by Seattle folk-singer-turned-eccentric-restaurateur Ivar Haglund (affectionately known to employees as "Our Flounder"), the establishment began as an aquarium that featured a fish and chips counter. By the mid-1940s, Haglund was focusing exclusively on his restaurant ambitions by opening Ivar's Acres of Clams. Using the self-created slogan "Keep Clam," Haglund grew his seafood business over the decades to include fish bars, drive-through restaurants and salmon houses in multiple locations throughout Washington. Visitors to the original Pier 54 location today can get a photo with a life-size statue of Ivar feeding fries to a quartet of hungry seagulls, something he encouraged patrons of his establishment to do from 1971 until his death in 1985.

A few slips north of Ivar's is Pier 57, known as Schwabacher's Wharf when it was first built in the 1890s. It was at this pier that the Japanese freighter *Miike Maru* first stopped in 1896, opening trade between Washington and the Land of the Rising Sun. It was also Schwabacher's Wharf that saw the arrival of the famed "Ship of Gold" in July 1897, which heralded the beginning of the Klondike gold rush that vaulted Seattle into global relevancy. The steamship *Portland*, returning from Canada's Yukon province, had telegraphed ahead to announce it would arrive laden with a massive amount of gold and sixty-eight rich miners. Crowds of thousands gathered on the wharf to welcome the ship and watch with awe and envy as crews unloaded the riches from the hold. The very next ship to leave for the Klondike carried hundreds of men, each hoping to return with a similar fortune.

So great was the demand for maritime transportation to the Yukon that a small company originally producing mining equipment soon turned its efforts to shipbuilding. The company, started by Robert Moran, became Moran Brothers Shipyards, one of the largest and most successful shipbuilders in the Pacific Northwest. It eventually produced over ninety steamships, battleships and submarines and established Robert Moran as an influential figure in early Washington business and politics.

The actual helm of the *Portland* is on display at MOHAI, and visitors to Seattle who really want to dive deep into the gold rush years can visit the Klondike Gold Rush National Historical Park at 319 Second Avenue S. in the former Cadillac Hotel building. Though the Klondike gold rush lasted only a few years, Schwabacher's Wharf (known as Pier 57 since 1902) lasted into the 1970s, when it was rebuilt and renamed. Visitors today can find the name "Miner's Landing" painted on the side in bright gold lettering, take in the sights and sounds from nearby Waterfront Park and enjoy a meal at one of several seafood restaurants. The truly daring can brave the heights of Seattle's Great Wheel or experience the thrills of the Wings over Washington ride—but there is little left on-site to tell the story of Pier 57's golden origins.

Continuing north along the waterfront, travelers will find the world-famous Seattle Aquarium atop Pier 59. Following a mission of inspiring conservation of the marine environment, Seattle Aquarium has been providing experiences and education in fun and fascinating ways since it opened in 1977. Patrons can learn about beach and ocean conservation, follow in the footsteps of marine scientists and see varied species of octopuses, otters and fish. Afterward, visitors may want to take a quiet stroll along the Waterfront Park at neighboring Pier 62.

HIRAM A. CHITTENDEN LOCKS

A marvel of engineering, the Chittenden Locks in Ballard (known locally as the Ballard Locks) allow marine traffic to pass between the freshwater Lake Washington, the sometimes-brackish Lake Union and the salty waters of Elliott Bay on Puget Sound. This is accomplished through a series of chambers, called locks, which can be opened and closed as boats move through the passage; the water level within each lock can be raised or lowered to equal that of the next stage. There is a passageway for small vessels, like kayaks and recreational boats, and one for large vessels, like cruise ships and commercial fishing boats. However, on busy summer days, travelers may find their eighteen-foot Bayliner floating right beside a monstrous cargo ship, as the locks—like any other transportation corridor—can experience marine traffic jams. Visitors to the century-old facility are invited to explore the grounds at no cost, watch the boats and ships rise and fall with the water levels, learn about the locks in the museum and visitor center and marvel at migrating salmon through the fish ladder windows.

Only three years after the first non-Native settlers took up residence in 1851, they began discussing ways to connect Lake Washington to Puget Sound. It must have seemed only natural to want a passageway between the freshwater lake and the salt water of Elliott Bay, which is only two and a half miles away at its narrowest point. Having that connection would have made it much easier to harvest and transport the inland's natural resources and prepare them for shipping, but the topography of the area proved more challenging than technology of the time could overcome.

It was roughly twenty more years before the Army Corps of Engineers concluded in a report that two passages would be needed, one for smaller ships and one for larger ones. The man who authored that report was Hiram A. Chittenden, head of the Army Corps Seattle District. Chittenden inherited the project from several predecessors, but it was his report that generated action. Many of his recommendations, such as using concrete locks instead of wooden ones and siting the final passageway between

Not only is the Hiram M. Chittenden Ballard Locks a national historic site, it is also among the busiest maritime navigation locks in the nation today. *Russ Heinl.*

Salmon Bay, connected to Lake Union, and Shilshole Bay on Puget Sound, were adopted for the final project.

On July 4, 1917, over half of Seattle's residents turned out for the grand opening festivities. The ship that ceremonially traversed the new locks was the SS *Roosevelt*, a steamer built to explore the Arctic. However, it wasn't the first ship to pass between salt and fresh water through Chittenden's creation. The locks had opened to marine traffic a year earlier, and the vast fleet of fishing and whaling vessels in Seattle almost immediately began mooring at Salmon Bay just inside the locks (soon after called Fishermen's Terminal). By one estimate, more than five thousand ships and boats had passed through the locks before the *Roosevelt*'s fanfare the following July.

There is a great deal more to the story of the Ballard Locks and their creation. Thankfully, there are several interpretive sites throughout the property. Visitors can tour the historic 1916 administration building, which still provides workspaces for employees; take a free guided tour of the grounds; or visit the museum, visitor center and gift shop, which are open at varying times throughout the year.

Fishermen's Terminal

Salmon Bay has long been home to working fishermen and women in Seattle, but its functional reputation shouldn't detract from its eligibility as a maritime destination. On the contrary, Fishermen's Terminal can be considered one of the state's "hidden gems" for history buffs and nautical enthusiasts alike. Boasting a number of restaurants, seafood markets and a collection of net sheds, warehouses and offices, Fishermen's Terminal is as much travel destination as it is working waterfront.

First opened in 1914, three years after the formation of the Port of Seattle, the docks on Salmon Bay—known then as Fishermen's Headquarters—provided a safe winter haven for hundreds of boats that had nowhere else to wait out the off-season. Several boat captains would even beach their vessels for the winter, leaving them at the mercy of the tides until fishing season returned. With the impending completion of the Chittenden Locks, however, the fishing community recognized the opportunity to create a permanent home for their boats while simultaneously adding to the economic vitality of the city.

Already, tens of millions of dollars' worth of seafood products were passing through Seattle, and port commissioners knew that if the fleet made the city their home port, Seattle would benefit from the dollars spent on vessel repairs, fuel and supplies. The commissioners drew up plans that included piers for fishing boats, cargo ships and ferries; warehouses to store fishing nets and gear in the off-season; machinery to haul boats in and out of the water; and office buildings.

As time passed, the port commissioners replaced dilapidated buildings with new ones, expanded the size of the terminal and installed new and more modern piers and amenities. Throughout the lifespan of Fishermen's Terminal, port commissioners have often reiterated the facility's importance not only as a home for fishing and other commercial vessels but also as a destination for visitors interested in Pacific Northwest maritime industries. The facility now caters to both commercial vessels and pleasure craft and provides free public moorage for visiting boats for up to four hours. Investing in both visions simultaneously has resulted in one of the most uniqely authentic waterfront attractions in Washington today.

Visitors can take a walking tour of the grounds, visiting several historically significant sites throughout the property. Shopping at one of several seafood markets can provide the absolute freshest of fish, or if patrons would rather have their fare prepared by talented chefs, they can grab a memorable meal

Fishermen have been inspecting and repairing nets at the Port of Seattle's Fishermen's Terminal on Salmon Bay for more than a century. *Seattle Municipal Archives #10525*.

at one of the facility's restaurants or cafés. If nothing else, guests should spend time in the memorial garden and at the Fishermen's Memorial, a bronze and stone sculpture inscribed with the names of hundreds of individuals who have lost their lives in pursuit of their livelihoods since the beginning of the twentieth century.

HUB CITY: EVERETT

Just north of Seattle and King County lies the city of Everett, named in honor of Everett Colby, the son of an East Coast investor who helped develop the city in 1892. Located between the Snohomish River and Possession Sound, what is now Everett has its own storied maritime history. The consortium of businessmen that platted Everett billed it as the "City of Smokestacks"—a moniker that was probably more appealing at the time than it sounds today—and intended it to become the "Pittsburgh of the West," both designations shared by multiple cities in Washington. Its location at the mouth of the Snohomish River made it an ideal location to site lumber mills, shipping operations, seafood harvesting and other industrial ventures that would ostensibly bring national significance to the city.

As with most plans for settlement in the Pacific Northwest, however, newcomers had to account for the Indigenous people already inhabiting the area. Members of the Snohomish Tribe lived in villages along the water and the Snohomish River, including the central village of Hibulb. Its location near the mouth of the river provided the tribe with resources, food and access to maritime transportation, but it was also a strategic location that allowed the tribe to keep watch over the waters for approaching raids. After the Treaty of Point Elliott in 1855, the Snohomish were relocated to a nearby reservation on Tulalip Bay (pronounced "tuh-LAY-lup," an anglicized version of the word dxʷlilap) along with members from several other tribes. Though the federal government continued to interact with each tribe separately, those tribes formed a tribal government around 1934 under the name Tulalip Tribes of Washington, also known as the People of the Salmon. The Salish word translates to "far to the end," in reference to how canoes had to swing wide when entering the bay to avoid the shallow water. In fact, there's evidence that when George Vancouver first sailed into the area in 1792, his own ship may have run aground on the sandbar.

Everett has a rich history worth exploring, and the destinations that can be reached from Everett within a day can provide visitors with even more maritime education and entertainment to enjoy. Naval Station Everett is situated right on the waterfront, and there are ferry terminals to nearby islands located in Mukilteo and Edmonds a few miles to the south.

Port of Everett

As the Snohomish Tribe well knew and the earliest non-Indian settlers soon discovered, the area where Everett is today was an ideal location for waterfront activity. Given the number of natural resources available, it was no surprise when residents formed the Port of Everett in 1918. With lumber and shingle mills springing up, the industrialists needed access to shipping opportunities. When World War II began, the port ramped up production and shipping of wood and timber for the war effort and relocated the steadily growing fishing fleet to a new area north of the original dock. This area eventually became the marina where today's recreational boaters can find moorage. And in 1986, the port sold over one hundred acres of its shipping property to the U.S. Navy to create the naval station that employs hundreds of sailors and civilians today.

From the historic working waterfront on the port's south end to the largest public boat launch in the state on the north end, the entirety of Everett's port property is peppered with interesting features for maritime enthusiasts, like the Port of Everett's Fisherman's Tribute Memorial and the foot ferry to Jetty Island. Located in the heart of the port at Fishermen's Tribute Plaza, the statue of a mariner hauling in a fishing net pays special homage to Everett's fishing industry and those who've lost their lives working at sea. Nearby is Jetty Landing, a vibrant park that doubles as a waiting area for pedestrians on their way to Jetty Island. The island was created naturally by a buildup of sediment deposited at the mouth of the Snohomish River, and city founders began improving the area as early as 1895 to create what is today a beautiful place for recreation and natural enjoyment. The island's natural sandy beaches are open year-round but are accessible only by watercraft. During Jetty Island Days (July 5 through Labor Day), the port operates a foot ferry, and reservations are required for the round-trip ticket.

HIBULB CULTURAL CENTER AND NATURAL HISTORY PRESERVE

A few miles north of Everett is an Indigenous attraction any visitor will enjoy. With a mission to revive, restore, protect, interpret, collect and enhance the history, traditional cultural values and spiritual beliefs of the Tulalip Tribes, the Hibulb Cultural Center and Natural History Preserve is a must-see for anyone interested the pre-contact history of the Snohomish (anglicized from sduhubš, or "Extraordinary People"), the Snoqualmie (anglicized from sdukʷalbixʷ, or "People of the Moon") and Skyomish (anglicized from sqʼíxʷəbš, or "Inland People"). The center, the first of its kind in Washington to be a fully certified collections and archaeological repository, features multiple interactive exhibits, classrooms, a traditional longhouse, a research library and more.

Some of the artifacts include textiles woven with wool harvested from the now-extinct woolly dog, a breed developed and bred by Coast Salish people. The wool was said to have produced luxurious blankets, highly coveted items that no doubt kept wearers warm on chilly nights when coastal Puget Sound winds whipped through villages. Another fascinating feature of the Hibulb Cultural Center is its stories told in both English and Lushootseed (anglicized from dxʷləšucid), one of nearly two dozen languages that make up the Salishan language family. Washington tribes from as far north as Bellingham to as far south as Olympia traditionally speak some dialect of Lushootseed, and the Tulalip Tribes are dedicated to reinstating awareness and usage of the language within their community and beyond. Visitors to the cultural center will no doubt experience a lasting memorable moment when hearing Lushootseed spoken fluently by cultural interpreters.

As with most Coast Salish tribes, canoes are of prime importance to the culture. In the center's Canoe Hall, guests can see examples of the types of canoes used by the Tulalip Tribes and learn more about the history and mythology of their people. Learn more about the rich heritage of the Tulalip Tribes at the Hibulb Cultural Center, 6410 Twenty-Third Avenue NE in Tulalip.

The grounds of today's Tulalip Resort Casino are highlighted with sculptures and images that hearken back to the tribe's maritime and cultural heritage. *Blake Handley.*

The city of Marysville to the north is home to the Tulalip Resort Casino, a tribal-owned hotel and gaming establishment decorated with an impressive array of Native artwork—much of it maritime-themed. In front of the resort, visitors will be awed by several life-size orca statues adorning the water feature along the entranceway. Among the cascading waterfalls and spraying fountains, guests can spot sculptures of leaping salmon and a tribal fisherman waiting by the water's edge amid beautiful gardens welcoming visitors to the modern facility.

BRACKETT'S LANDING SHORELINE SANCTUARY

South of Everett is the city of Edmonds, a onetime timber town that has reinvented itself as a vibrant cultural destination. Home to an impressive array of recreational activities like musical events, performing arts shows, food and beverage options, a public fishing pier, nature walks, birdwatching and beachcombing, Edmonds also has a terminal for the ferry to Kingston, just across Puget Sound on the Kitsap Peninsula. In fact, the beaches flanking the ferry dock happen to be the site where town founder George Brackett is said to have first set foot in the area. The Ballard resident had been paddling north along the saltwater shoreline looking for stands of virgin timber when his canoe blew ashore during a windstorm in 1870. The site was ripe for harvesting, and a few years later, he purchased the land and resettled his family. After draining the marshland, Brackett began logging the area, and it eventually attracted more settlers to the growing community. When the time came for the area to officially become a city, Brackett was elected its first mayor.

Known today as Brackett's Landing, the former industrial area was reimagined and renovated in the 1970s to become a veritable playground for maritime enthusiasts. The northern and southern beaches offer over a mile of shoreline to explore, walking paths dotted with ocean-themed sculptures, a public fishing pier and picnic areas where visitors can watch ferries come in and out. Subtly adding to the ambiance are rows of old pilings disappearing into the sea as if retreating from a bygone era.

Brackett's Landing on the Edmonds waterfront is named for the city's founder, George Brackett, who bought 147 acres of virgin timberland near the shore in 1872. *Joe Mabel.*

One of the most notable attractions at Brackett's Landing (besides the spectacular sunsets) is the Edmonds Marine Sanctuary just offshore. Set aside for protection in the 1970s, the sanctuary is home to hundreds of aquatic species. It is also an extremely popular dive park, so if visitors happen to bring scuba gear, they can swim among the sanctuary's rockfish and eelgrass. Those wanting the experience but finding themselves without proper equipment can easily find rental and instruction opportunities in town. The dive park and marine sanctuary are considered a "no-take" zone, meaning visitors are asked not to remove shells, rocks, animals or any other natural souvenir, and the waters off Brackett's Landing are closed to boats of any kind—including kayaks and stand-up paddleboards—and dogs must be always leashed.

Mukilteo Lighthouse Park

Between Edmonds and Everett is the city of Mukilteo (anglicized from bəqˈltiyuʔ and pronounced "muckle-TEE-oh"), the eastern gateway to Whidbey Island. One of the more affluent communities in western Washington, Mukilteo had been the site of a Snohomish village for the better part of a millennium before settlement by non-Indians began around 1853. The Lushootseed name translates to either "good camping ground," "long goose neck" or "narrow passage," depending on the source. When the Vancouver expedition landed in 1792, the area was named Rose Point on account of the wild roses that blanketed the hillside. The Wilkes expedition later renamed the site Elliott Point after one of the crew members. It wasn't until 1860 that town founders renamed the community in deference to its Indigenous beginnings.

One of the most enjoyable maritime attractions in Mukilteo is its lighthouse and surrounding grounds. Known as Mukilteo Lighthouse Park, the main feature is the century-old lighthouse at 609 Front Street. Built in 1906 and claimed, at the time, to be the best lighthouse on Puget Sound, the structure housed an 1852 fourth-order Fresnel lens that could cast its light ten miles across the water. The station also included a trumpet-shaped foghorn that blasted its warning in four-second bursts every sixteen seconds. Added to the National Register of Historic Places in 1977, the lighthouse was renovated several times through the years and finally automated in 1979. Up to that point, eighteen lighthouse keepers and their families had been tasked with

Mukilteo Lighthouse Park, constructed in the 1950s near the Whidbey Island ferry terminal, is home to a historic light station and keeper's quarters built in 1906. *Washington Our Home.*

overseeing operations at the facility—a coveted assignment on account of its enviable location and on-site amenities.

Visitors to the park today can tour the grounds, learning about the history of the lighthouse thanks to the efforts of the Mukilteo Historical Society, as well as traverse the ADA-accessible shoreline walkway, take a self-guided walking tour through the park or enjoy the spectacular views from one of a dozen picnic tables. Beachcombers can stroll the waterfront, and boaters can make use of the public launch, while anglers can take advantage of the public fishing pier. After building up an appetite, be sure to stop by Ivar's Fish Bar just north of the park or enjoy the fare at several other drinking and dining establishments nearby.

HUB CITY: BREMERTON

The city of Bremerton in Kitsap County is named in honor of German immigrant and Seattle entrepreneur William Bremer, who planned the city in 1891. Bremerton lies in picturesque Sinclair Inlet, named after a member of the Wilkes expedition and home to many varieties of birds and marine mammals. The community's role as the center of activity for the entire Kitsap Peninsula has prompted it to heavily invest in its waterfront area. Visitors in warmer weather can cool off at the Harborside Fountains—a splash park at 251 First Street that features water-erupting sculptures strongly resembling submarine sail towers—or stroll over a quarter mile of public pier from which anglers can catch crab, rockfish and other saltwater delicacies.

The ferry terminal at Bremerton is one of the larger and more modern in the state, staging travelers heading to and from Seattle. There are also ferries that take walk-on passengers across the inlet to Port Orchard and Annapolis. The waterfront boardwalk guides visitors past the Kitsap Conference Center and the Port of Bremerton Marina, which offers over three hundred slips for moorage. Multiple shops, restaurants, hotels and cafés line the waterfront as well, and explorers interested in the history of Bremerton or the surrounding area can visit the Kitsap History Museum at 280 Fourth Street just a few blocks from the waterfront.

Puget Sound Naval Shipyard and Navy Museum

Bremerton features a lot of maritime history but perhaps none so visible as the Puget Sound Naval Shipyard. William Bremer knew the U.S. Navy was searching for a suitable location to site a naval base. Once the rumors were proven true, Bremer purchased 170 acres from a homesteader where he figured the base would be built. In 1891, the navy bought 81 acres from Bremer, who then turned around and filed a plat to build a town on some of the remaining property. While the navy began developing its new base on Puget Sound, Bremer went about creating a town to support it.

Until 1916, what was known as Navy Yard Puget Sound had been a repair and maintenance facility. With two granite and concrete dry docks capable of handling some of the largest marine vessels in the world, the shipyard should have been well positioned to support the war effort when the United States entered World War I. However, as the yard was located on the far side of the country, the navy opted instead to change its mission to shipbuilding. During the Great War, Navy Yard Puget Sound churned out two minesweepers, two ammunition ships, six submarines, seven ocean tugs, twenty-five submarine chasers and nearly two thousand smaller boats.

For several decades after World War I, the federal government continued to invest heavily in its shipyard on Sinclair Inlet. In 1933, crews installed an enormous hammerhead crane to help streamline the shipbuilding process. By the 1940s, Navy Yard Puget Sound boasted five dry docks and employed over thirty thousand people. At the onset of America's entry into World War II, the facility's mission shifted again to maintenance and repair, servicing the country's Pacific battle fleet. Between 1941 and 1945, sailors stationed at the yard worked on over five hundred ships—including eighteen aircraft carriers, thirteen cruisers and seventy-nine destroyers. Despite the change in mission, workers also built another fifty-three ships during that time in support of the American cause.

When the war ended, the navy officially changed the facility's name to Puget Sound Naval Shipyard and began focusing its efforts on the deactivation and dismantling of the Pacific Fleet. Some of the ships were kept in special environments, a practice known as "mothballing," to preserve them for future use, which occurred during the Korean War. The shipyard continued modernizing some of the more useful ships in the navy, mothballing others for which they might have a need later and deactivating those well past their prime, such as the USS *Missouri*, aboard

Founded in 1891, the Puget Sound Naval Shipyard built ships during World War I, repaired ships during World War II and was designated a National Historic Landmark in 1992. *Public domain.*

which the United States accepted Japan's formal surrender to the Allied Powers in Tokyo Bay on September 2, 1945.

During the 1980s and '90s, Puget Sound Naval Shipyard was commended for finding ways to dismantle nuclear-powered ships and submarines safely and environmentally, winning several national awards. Today, the facility— over 130 years old—continues to succeed in its mission, employing a formidable force of mechanics, engineers, architects, welders, scientists, electricians, machinists, painters, pipefitters, riggers, shipwrights and more. The shipyard still answers America's call to service daily, which is why— despite being listed as a National Historic Landmark District in 1992—it cannot allow tourists to visit the facility under most circumstances.

Fortunately for military and maritime enthusiasts, nestled snugly between Puget Sound Naval Shipyard's eastern property line and the beautiful Bremerton waterfront boardwalk is the Puget Sound Navy Museum at 251 First Street, just north of the splash park. Operating out of the historic Building 50, relocated from the shipyard next door, the museum features the sail of the Sturgeon-class nuclear submarine USS *Parche* in its beautiful memorial plaza at the building's entrance. Inside, visitors are greeted by a magnificent interpretive display of the Puget Sound's naval facilities. The museum tells the storied history of the shipyard as well as several vessels that have called it home over the years.

A permanent exhibit on the USS *Nimitz* aircraft carrier, one of the largest warships in the world, takes visitors on an educational adventure through the heart of the vessel and the diverse company of navy men and women who served aboard. Guests may also find exhibits dedicated to some of the more unknown aspects of U.S. Navy history, like the research and development of hydrofoil patrol and gunboats, unofficial navy traditions, tattoos in nautical culture and women of the shipyard. The Puget Sound Navy Museum is free, but parking near the building is limited, so look for street options nearby.

USS *Turner Joy*

Maritime explorers walking the length of Bremerton's waterfront boardwalk will pass an impressive sculpture commemorating the first one hundred years of the Puget Sound Naval Shipyard, featuring a worker and a child looking at a model ship in front of a giant propeller. Just a little farther, the boardwalk leads right to one of the most fascinating sights a naval afficionado could ask for: the Vietnam War–era destroyer-turned-museum-ship USS *Turner Joy*.

Built by the Puget Sound Bridge and Dredging Company of Seattle, the Forrest Sherman–class destroyer launched in May 1958 as part of the post–World War II modernization of America's military. The ship is most well known for its part in the Gulf of Tonkin incident in 1964, a precursor to escalating American involvement in Vietnam.

Turner Joy spent nine years fighting for the American cause during the Vietnam War and another nine years in peacetime operations around the world. When the navy decommissioned the ship in 1982, it was sent to the Inactive Ships Reserve Fleet in Bremerton for storage. In the late 1980s, when the city learned it would likely be losing its iconic Reserve Fleet vessel, the battleship USS *Missouri* (to become part of the Pearl Harbor Memorial in Hawaii), city leaders sought another navy vessel to take its place as a tourist and economic attraction. The nonprofit Bremerton Historic Ships Association selected the four-hundred-foot *Turner Joy* to become both a naval memorial museum ship on the Bremerton waterfront as well as a

Commissioned in 1959, the USS *Turner Joy* was named for Admiral Charles Turner Joy and is now the Bremerton Naval Memorial on the city's waterfront. It is one of eighteen U.S. Navy Forrest Sherman–class destroyers and was built in Seattle. *Washington Our Home.*

breakwater for the Bremerton Marina next to the ferry terminal. In 1990, the association asked the navy to donate the *Turner Joy* to its custody, and the request was approved.

Visitors can explore the USS *Turner Joy*—the only one of its kind on Puget Sound—on their own or take advantage of one of the onboard docents who provide guests with guided tours. The ship is ADA compliant on the main deck, and there are several wheelchairs on hand for less mobile visitors. *Turner Joy* often welcomes navy-related groups and naval reunions, and tours can last anywhere from a brisk thirty-minute review to a multi-hour, in-depth inspection of each bulkhead and battery, hatch and halyard.

U.S. NAVAL UNDERSEA MUSEUM

The U.S. Navy's presence in Kitsap County isn't limited to the shipyard and museum in Bremerton. Ten miles to the northwest is Naval Base Kitsap, a huge swath of land along Hood Canal on the peninsula's western edge. Originally an ammunition storage and shipping depot for the World War II effort when it was constructed near Bangor in 1942, the facility expanded its footprint dramatically three years later. The navy purchased over seven thousand acres to create Naval Support Base Bangor, which stored and supplied conventional weapons to the U.S. fleet for another thirty years.

In 1973, the navy announced it was converting the facility into a base for its new Ohio-class Trident ballistic missile submarines, changing the name of the facility to Naval Submarine Base Bangor. Crews stationed there provided maintenance, calibration, assembly and testing and nuclear warhead storage for Trident submarines and the ballistic missiles that they were capable of launching. The base's location was ideal due to the depth of Hood Canal, which averages 177 feet but reaches a maximum depth of over 600 feet. A lucky few Washingtonians have had the experience of gazing peacefully across the water, only to see the placid channel suddenly begin churning into a froth of bubbles before an enormous submarine dramatically breached the surface.

After the turn of the millennium, the navy merged Naval Base Bangor and Naval Base Bremerton, creating today's Naval Base Kitsap. However, directly east of the base is another navy facility with a specific purpose in Keyport, Washington. Originally called the Pacific Coast Torpedo Station, the often-overlooked maritime facility has been a part of Washington since before World War I. Known since 1992 as the Naval Undersea Warfare Center (NUWC), Keyport Division, it is the only one of its kind on the Pacific Ocean—the other being in Newport, Rhode Island.

NUWC Keyport provides the U.S. Navy with technical leadership, engineering expertise and unique facilities to keep America at the forefront of undersea warfare technology. When self-propelled torpedoes became a growing threat after the Spanish-American War, the navy began investing in facilities to improve its capabilities in underwater combat. Submarines on the West Coast, however, had to ship their torpedoes to Rhode Island for testing, maintenance and repair. To remedy this costly problem, the navy purchased land in 1914 near its base in Kitsap County and opened the Pacific Coast Torpedo Station. There, the navy began stationing divers, engineers, technicians, security personnel and a small civilian workforce tasked with testing and maintaining torpedoes for the Pacific Fleet.

With each successive military conflict, the station continued to prove its value. With an expanding mission and added responsibilities came new designations for the facility. It was renamed the U.S. Naval Torpedo Station in

U.S. Navy sailors tend the mooring lines of the ballistic-missile submarine *Maine* (SSBN-741) at Bangor, Washington, near Bremerton. *USN photo #N-9204H-107 by Chief Mass Communication Specialist Eric Harrison.*

1930, the Naval Undersea Warfare Engineering Station in 1978 and finally, the NUWC in 1992. Today, the division has detachments in California, Hawaii, Nevada, Guam, Japan and Canada and is a critical component of the U.S. military's operational readiness.

Fortunately, just outside the NUWC main gate in Keyport is another, more public facility to help interpret the long history of underwater naval operations. The U.S. Naval Undersea Museum is unmissable thanks to the enormous underwater research vessels staged across the parking lot from the prominent sail of the USS *Sturgeon* next to the main entrance. Without question, it is one of the most unique museums in Washington, holding the most comprehensive collection of U.S. Navy documents and artifacts related to torpedoes, mines, diving and salvage operations, submarine technology and undersea vehicles in the country.

Visitors can learn how torpedo technology evolved and see the inner workings of some of the world's first versions or sit at the controls of the nuclear submarine USS *Greenling*, hearing radio calls and watching enemy ships approaching on glowing sonar display. Guests can explore the history of naval rescue and recovery operations from 1900 through today or learn what makes naval mines such an effective weapon, responsible for sinking more ships than anything else in the past century. The museum also features content on the oceanic environment and its key physical properties, such as buoyancy, pressure, density and oxygen.

Admission to the U.S. Naval Undersea Museum, located at 1 Garnett Way in Keyport, is free.

Poulsbo Maritime Museum

Farther up the Kitsap Peninsula is the delightful city of Poulsbo. Usually pronounced "PAULS-bo," this seaside community is also known as "Little Norway," as it was founded in the 1880s by Norwegian loggers, farmers and anglers. The town has cherished its Nordic heritage for over a century, as evidenced by the vast number of Scandinavian-themed restaurants, bakeries and boutiques. Situated at the northern tip of Liberty Bay, Poulsbo has long been a haven for boats seeking safe harbor during the off-season.

When the first non-Indigenous settlers arrived in the area, they found the climate and topography like that of their home countries and immediately set about creating a way of life. One of those early settlers, Iver Brynildsen Moe, suggested the community be named after his hometown of Paulsbo, Norway, but a likely misreading of the 1886 post office application resulted in the current spelling of Poulsbo. Regardless, life in the growing marine community flourished as more Nordic immigrants began relocating there. In fact, Norwegian was the primary language in Poulsbo until World War II, when the navy built housing in the community for workers at the shipyard in Bremerton.

Though its earliest days saw the development of logging mills and timber businesses, the early twentieth century was marked by a wave of Norwegian fishermen moving to Liberty Bay—then known as Dogfish Bay. Soon, the Pacific Coast Codfish Company set up shop in Poulsbo on the insistence of investor Iver Moe. The company bought a fleet of schooners from the lumber mills and converted them to hold fish, then sailed them to Alaska where the cod fishing was best. The voyage took about a month, but the effort resulted in a haul of over one hundred thousand fish per ship.

As Poulsbo grew, so did the fishing fleet and its ability to bring in cod. As the ships returned at the end of each season, crews emptied their holds

Poulsbo, Washington, has historically been the base of operations for hundreds of fishing vessels, which often travel as far north as the rich waters off the coast of Alaska. *Nick Hoke*.

at the Pacific Coast Codfish Company's processing plant. Traditionally, these Scandinavians used salt to preserve their catch, but the development of refrigeration technology soon eliminated the need for that method. The company finally closed its doors permanently in the 1950s, but the fishing industry has never abandoned Poulsbo entirely. Though pleasure boats vastly outnumber working fishing boats in the Poulsbo Marina today, many commercial fishing outfits still call Liberty Bay their home port.

One of the best ways a history buff can appreciate Poulsbo is by visiting the Maritime Museum and Heritage Museum, next door to each other at 19010 and 19020 Front Street NE. At the Heritage Museum, explorers should not be surprised if they are greeted by a docent speaking Norwegian and may even learn a few unfamiliar words as they peruse the collection of items showcasing the many facets of life in the evolution of the community.

The Maritime Museum focuses exclusively on the nautical nature of Poulsbo and the northern Kitsap Peninsula. It features exhibits on the Pacific Coast Codfish Company and other maritime industries, the cod fishermen and the boats on which they lived and worked and the waterborne transportation methods used throughout history to reach Poulsbo, from the boat rowed by Nordic pioneers Jørgen Eliason and Peter Olson to the beloved Mosquito Fleet steamship *Hyak*. Residents of Poulsbo relied on the *Hyak* for fast travel to and from Seattle's Pier 54 from 1909 through 1937, when it was quietly retired. In fact, between the two museums is a replica of the *Hyak*'s pilothouse, where would-be captains can grasp the helm and gaze past Sons of Norway Hall at the marina on Liberty Bay in the distance, imagining what it would have been like to ferry passengers to the big city during that storied era.

The Suquamish People and Old Man House

Poulsbo and other communities on the Kitsap Peninsula are home to the Suquamish (anglicized from suq̓ʷabš and pronounced "suh-KWAM-ish"), or "People of Clear Salt Water." The Suquamish have existed for thousands of years and are a federally recognized tribe with tribal sovereignty, legal status and relations with the U.S. government.

The Suquamish are experts at building canoes, fishing and weaving, and they enjoy a rich cultural and spiritual life. Like other tribes in the Puget Sound region, the Suquamish moved seasonally throughout the spring, summer and fall to access fish, shellfish, game and plant resources. Three important men led the Suquamish people in their historic period, including Kitsap (anglicized from q'cap), who brought families together as a cohesive social group and helped establish the Suquamish people as respected members of the region's economic and social systems. Kitsap was a warrior who led the Suquamish and other tribes against raiding parties from Alaska and Vancouver Island, as well as a spiritual leader with knowledge of healing powers. Early settlers named Kitsap County after this Suquamish leader.

When George Vancouver anchored his ships off Bainbridge Island's Restoration Point in 1792, the notes he made included the first historical references to the Suquamish Tribe. By the 1820s, the Suquamish were trading with members of the Hudson's Bay Company, and from the 1820s through the 1840s, it was Challacum (anglicized from čələq'um) who led the Suquamish people. A well-known trading partner with the Hudson's Bay Company, Challacum traveled regularly by canoe between Fort Nisqually, near today's DuPont, and Fort Langley, near Vancouver, British Columbia. When Charles Wilkes sailed into Puget Sound in 1841, he made numerous descriptions of Suquamish villages and camps on the Olympic and Kitsap Peninsulas.

The third leader, Seattle, was an entrepreneur and political leader who encouraged non-Indian settlers to establish stores, lumber mills and other economic enterprises on Elliott Bay, helping cement his position as the lead Indian signatory of the Treaty of Point Elliott in 1855. The Suquamish people's "mother village" was on Agate Passage, across from the north end of Bainbridge Island. Kitsap, Challacum and Seattle's father, Schweabe (anglicized from šxʷiyiʔhəb), constructed a large cedar-plank building that became known as Old Man House, an anglicization of the Chinook Jargon word o'-le-man. The structure was between fifty and one hundred feet wide and over eight hundred feet long. It housed numerous families and was well known for hosting large gatherings of Indian people from throughout the region during spiritual events and economic exchanges known as potlatches.

Just over a decade after Wilkes's arrival, the U.S. government appointed Isaac Stevens to govern Washington Territory. As American settlers made land claims and constructed buildings on traditional Indian villages and resource-gathering locations, conflicts arose between the newcomers and Indian people. Stevens, in his dual role as governor and superintendent of Indian affairs, recommended the U.S. government sign treaties with the Indigenous people that had them cede their lands and move to reservations while retaining rights to fish, hunt, collect plants and harvest shellfish in their usual and accustomed areas.

As the designated "principal chief," Seattle made certain the Treaty of Point Elliott established a reservation for his people in the heart of their ancestral homeland. As part of the government's assimilation program, Suquamish families were encouraged to move from the communal Old Man House to small, single-family cabins. By 1868, most families in the village had their own houses, and only a few structural elements of Old Man House remained. Two years later, designated a health and safety hazard by the U.S. Indian Agency, Old Man House was set ablaze and reduced to ashes. Today, in the town of Suquamish, Old Man House Park encompasses a portion of where the longhouse once stood.

The Suquamish people have witnessed many changes to their traditional way of life over the past two centuries, but it hasn't crushed their spirit. If anything, it has awakened within them a stronger desire to see their culture flourish once again. To help achieve that goal, the tribe built the aptly named House of Awakened Culture in 2009 as a modern adaptation of a traditional longhouse. It is a place to learn and celebrate Suquamish heritage through

The remains of Old Man House, reportedly one of the longest winter Big Houses in the Salish Sea. Even after its destruction, Suquamish people camped at the site where it was located. *Suquamish Museum Archives, circa 1875.*

Lushootseed language classes, weaving, carving, dancing, singing and more. A short walk from the House of Awakened Culture is the Suquamish Dock, reminiscent of the Mosquito Fleet pier that once welcomed visitors regularly to Suquamish. The new dock provides access to the water for both tribal members and guests and is a great place from which to view the beauty of Port Madison.

THE PORT GAMBLE S'KLALLAM TRIBE

A charming destination on the Kitsap Peninsula, the quaint seaside village of Port Gamble is located just west of the Hood Canal Bridge. It was known as Teekalet when town founders first arrived in 1853 and built a sawmill to harvest the plentiful timber resources in the area. Of course, the S'Klallam people (anglicized from nəxʷsƛ̓áy̓əm) had been living there for generations but agreed to relocate across the mouth of the bay to make way for what became the Puget Mill Company.

After only a few years, Teekalet became a thriving mill town in need of more workers—and the S'Klallam Tribe had been relegated by the 1855 Treaty of Point No Point to a reservation much farther south along Hood Canal. Not interested in relocating again, the tribe continued to reside across from the mill at Point Julia, a place that became known as Little Boston. Some gained employment in the mill, canoeing across the bay twice a day to work.

After 142 years of continuous operation, the mill at Port Gamble—at that point, the oldest continuously operating sawmill in the country—closed for good in 1995. After some strategic realignment, Port Gamble began attracting new business and tourist activities while maintaining its historical buildings, creating the quiet getaway destination it is today. On the other side of the bay, the Port Gamble S'Klallam Tribe (anglicized from nəxʷqíyt nəxʷsX̣ʼáyʼəm) has also reinvented itself. Suffering the loss of 438,430 acres of homeland to poorly negotiated, misunderstood treaty negotiations left the tribe facing a monumental challenge to its existence. However, after the Fish Wars of the 1960s and the reaffirmation of their treaty rights by the Boldt Decision in 1974, the Port Gamble S'Klallam banded with several neighboring tribes to create a fisheries management council to improve fishing resources in the area.

In the decades that followed, the tribe built a fish hatchery, a gas station and a business park on their reservation. They soon created an economic development strategy and began administering federal grant funding, creating an inviting business climate for enterprises such as the Gliding Eagle Market, the Point Casino and Hotel (7989 NE Salish Lane in Kingston) and the Noo-Kayet Development Corporation. Members of the tribe today continue to hunt, fish and dig for clams in the same areas as their ancestors, while working to rejuvenate their people's rich canoe culture and Salish way of life.

POINT NO POINT

Near the northern tip of Kitsap County is a small outcropping of land rich with state and maritime history. Originally known as Hahdskus by the area's Native tribes, it was renamed by Wilkes in 1841. He noted that the point appeared to be substantial from a distance, yet on closer inspection, he realized that it was but a small spit of land and subsequently called it

Point No Point. Fourteen years later, Governor Isaac Stevens would use the land at Point No Point as a gathering place for some 1,200 members of the S'Klallam, Skokomish and Chimakum Tribes to hear and ultimately sign what became known as the Point No Point Treaty. As with the other treaties Stevens brought to the area's Indigenous peoples, there was no room for negotiation.

The treaty was read in limited Chinook Jargon to a gathering of some 1,200 Indians, and interpreters waited as the tribes discussed it among themselves. Several of them gave eloquent speeches bemoaning their proposed loss of land, wondering aloud where they would find food or bury their dead. They informed Stevens and his men that they wished to consider the weighty matter overnight, to which the governor agreed. The following morning, the tribes returned bearing white flags of truce and signed the treaty.

According to the treaty's provisions, the S'Klallam and Chimakum people were given one year to move with the Skokomish onto a reservation at the southernmost point of Hood Canal, the territory of the Skokomish but a significant distance from the traditional lands of the other two tribes. In addition, the tribes were to be paid about $60,000 and permitted to continue fishing in their usual and accustomed grounds—a pivotal point in the 1974 lawsuit that ended the Fish Wars by upholding tribal fishing rights.

By 1879, the U.S. Lighthouse Service had constructed a lighthouse at Point No Point in anticipation of increased marine traffic after the Northern Pacific Railroad reached its western terminus at Tacoma, Washington. By that time, the spit of land had already been the cause of numerous shipwrecks after captains navigated their vessels too close to the shoal, and a light and fog signal at that location would help prevent future groundings in the shallow water. As there were no roads leading to the point, all construction materials—as well as materials for a lighthouse keeper's residence and related sundry items—had to be shipped in by boat. It wasn't until 1893 that Norwegian homesteaders began congregating near the light station, eventually naming the settlement Hansville after one of its residents.

The expectation of increased marine traffic was well founded, as more ships began rounding past the point in subsequent years. While incidents of ships running aground dwindled thanks to the lighthouse, it didn't put an end to shipwrecks entirely. In 1914, the *Princess Victoria* collided with the SS *Admiral Sampson* in heavy fog, nearly cleaving the *Admiral Sampson* in two. Both ships were filled with passengers, and most of those from the *Admiral Sampson* were able to jump aboard the deck of the *Princess Victoria* before watching the steamship disappear beneath the dark water. Sadly, eleven passengers, four crew members and the captain of the *Admiral Sampson* died in the disaster. The heavily damaged *Princess Victoria* continued to Seattle with a fourteen-foot gash across its bow.

In later years, management of the Point No Point lighthouse passed to the U.S. Coast Guard, which kept the station staffed until 1997. The lighthouse is on both the Washington Heritage Register as well as the National Register of Historic Places. Once the lighthouse buildings became obsolete, Kitsap County leased the property from the Coast Guard and made plans to develop the area as a maritime destination.

Today, Point No Point is a sixty-one-acre park operated by Kitsap County. Visitors can enjoy hiking through the area's marine wetlands, beachcombing, surf fishing, kite flying, picnicking, wildlife watching and, of course, learning about the history of the oldest lighthouse in the state as well as the point of land on which it sits. The historic lighthouse keeper's residence has been converted into a duplex and is available as a rental property through the U.S. Lighthouse Society, a nonprofit organization that manages the buildings.

Point No Point Lighthouse, circa 1970. The vast wetland behind it likely served as the site of the Point No Point Treaty signing in 1855. *Public domain.*

There is one more hidden gem of note. On route to Point No Point Lighthouse Park, located at 9009 NE Point No Point Road in Hansville, visitors may notice a house unlike any most have ever seen, one that any maritime enthusiast is sure to appreciate—even envy. At first glance, the two-story home might be mistaken for part of a retired ferry, but this structure is in fact the wheelhouse of a U.S. Maritime Commission Type V seagoing tug, complete with portholes, a foremast and crow's nest, a flying bridge and open bridge wings. Once known as the M/V *Jupiter Inlet*, the house today sits quietly nestled along the road to the Point No Point lighthouse.

The house's eccentric but unassuming nature belies its history as one of only forty-nine of the largest and most powerful tugs of its time, each named after lighthouses and built by six different shipyards in 1943 to aid the war effort. According to an interpretive sign in front of the home, these tugs were primarily used to move the rapidly growing number of merchant marine vessels, but some of them shepherded enormous concrete barges and docks across the Atlantic to help create a port for the D-Day landing at Normandy, France. The M/V *Jupiter Inlet* house is a brilliant example of how Washingtonians love maritime history, so be sure to stop by, read the interpretive signage and consider dropping a few coins in the donation box to help the owner keep it maintained.

PART II

NORTH
PUGET SOUND

Whatcom, Skagit, Island
and San Juan Counties

HUB CITY: BELLINGHAM

Far to the northern end of Washington's coastline lies the city of Bellingham in Whatcom County, incorporated in 1903 after the merging of four neighboring settlements. Named after Sir William Bellingham, the British navy storekeeper who supplied the Vancouver expedition, the city today is a thriving hot spot for heritage and the arts, lively outdoor activities, dining, shopping and more. Known as much for its maritime as its mountainous opportunities, Bellingham is also home to Central Washington University and the Bellingham Cruise Terminal, which offers connections to the San Juan Islands as well as a direct ferry to Ketchikan, Alaska.

True to its maritime origins, Bellingham holds an annual event called SeaFeast, a waterfront and seafood festival that jointly celebrates fishing industries, seafood cooking, working waterfronts and maritime heritage. Usually held in the fall, the popular community favorite attracts thousands of visitors and vendors each year.

Port of Bellingham

The Port of Bellingham is home to a vast collection of maritime businesses, including boat manufacturing and repair shops, marine suppliers, dive services, commercial fishing operations and charter vessels. Along with the various commercial activities, the Port of Bellingham properties include

A Whatcom County resident in the 1980s watches as crews construct the Port of Bellingham's Squalicum Harbor Marina atop old pilings leftover from a bygone era. *Port of Bellingham.*

several public parks, marinas, a U.S. Coast Guard station and a Marine Life Center dedicated to educating visitors about the myriad creatures that make their home in the Salish Sea. Located at 1801 Roeder Avenue in Squalicum Harbor, the Marine Life Center features interpretive signage, on-site educational specialists and numerous touch tanks that allow up-close-and-personal interaction with marine species like anemones, limpets, crabs, sea stars and more. It's open only by appointment, however, so travelers should call ahead before bringing the family for a visit.

While visiting Squalicum Harbor, travelers have their choice of bars, shops and restaurants to enjoy before stretching their legs walking the shoreline trail to Zuanich Point Park at 2600 Harbor Loop. Within the park is a community meeting center called the Squalicum Harbor Boathouse, as well as two monuments to the maritime industry. The original marker, known as the Fishermen's Memorial, was created in 1974 by the Puget Sound Gillnetters Women's Auxiliary. As the story goes, a local fisherman's net got caught on a rusty submerged anchor, which did considerable damage to the ship as it was hauled aboard. That anchor—thought to be a remnant of a historical British exploring expedition—is now on display at the park, along with the names of Bellingham fishermen who never made it home from their last voyage. Directly across the park stands the Safe Return monument, a pedestaled statue of a rope-wielding mariner going about the course of his duties. It, too, is adorned with names of Bellingham sailors either missing or deceased. It's a sobering reminder of just how dangerous the maritime trades can be.

Salmon Woman at Maritime Heritage Park

Traveling southwest along the New Waterfront Trail will lead explorers toward Maritime Heritage Park at 500 West Holly Street. Nestled between downtown Bellingham and the Whatcom Creek Waterway, the public park features a fish hatchery, an expansive amphitheater, a native plant trail and a salmon art trail. Though its name suggests otherwise, there is a notable absence of interpretive signage or heritage markers related specifically to maritime activities. However, there are two areas of the park that have a direct connection to Washington's seafaring heritage.

Atop the stairways cascading through the amphitheater in the center of the park are four sculptures created by artist Phillip Baldwin in 2000. Called *Four Ages of the Seas*, the aluminum silhouettes represent four different types of vessels that have been integral to the history of the area. Deeper in the park stands a carved wooden pole near the site where an ancient Native American village once existed. The pole, created by master carver Dale Jensen, depicts the story of Salmon Woman and Raven. It is a tale told for generations by the Lhaq'temish, or "People of the Sea," an Indigenous nation composed of the Lummi (anglicized from Xwlemi) and Sq 'elqx 'en descendants.

There are several versions of the story, each with minor differences in the details, but the main theme is the same. A long time ago, Raven was leading the Lhaq'temish people around their territory looking for sustenance. Finding no animals to hunt, berries to collect or roots to dig, Raven feared his people would soon starve. Intent on feeding his people, Raven set out in a canoe with no food of his own to explore the waters. He explored all the islands his people were familiar with, checking and rechecking places where food was once plentiful. Days went by with nothing to show for the searching.

By now, Raven was getting desperate. As a cold fog obscured any chance of finding his way home, Raven began preparing for his own death by singing about his coming journey between worlds. Salmon Woman heard his mournful song and took pity on him. She pretended to be a human struggling in the water so that Raven would come and rescue her. When he did, he wrapped her in a cedar mat and gave her the little water he had left. Moved by his generosity, Salmon Woman offered her own children—Chinook, Coho, Sockeye, Pink, Chum and Steelhead—to feed Raven and his people.

When they returned to the village, Raven married Salmon Woman, and the people were overjoyed at the abundance of salmon on which they could survive. But as time wore on, Salmon Woman saw that the people began taking her gift for granted and soon had enough of their disrespect. While Raven was away hunting, Salmon Woman took her children and returned to the waters whence they came. The people began to starve again and begged Raven to find his wife and her children.

After many days and nights searching, Raven found Salmon Woman and pleaded with her to return to the village. She eventually agreed, but under certain conditions. Her children would no longer make their homes in the river year-round but would return to the village once a year while traveling between their home in the ocean and their beds upriver. After this, the people lived harmoniously with the children of Salmon Woman and made sure to honor their sacrifice with a First Salmon Ceremony each season.

Whatcom Museum

One of the places visitors can learn more about the maritime history of the Lummi Nation is at the Whatcom Museum. Overlooking Maritime Heritage Park is the historic city hall building, one of three museum buildings within a one-block radius. Built in 1892, Old City Hall was the first building in Washington placed on the National Register of Historic Places. The exhibits within offer a comprehensive history of the pioneer settlement of areas throughout Whatcom County, including its maritime heritage. Visitors can learn about steamships, fisheries, schooners and more through photographs, artifacts, models and interactive experiences.

The museum, located at 121 Prospect Street in Bellingham, also features a wealth of historical information about the Lummi and other Indigenous

A Lummi tribal fisherman shows off the five-pound wild king salmon he harvested near Bellingham, Washington. *USDA.*

peoples of the area. After signing the Treaty of Point Elliott in 1855, the Lummi Tribe settled onto a reservation of about 12,500 acres—much smaller than their original hunting and fishing territory, which extended from Whatcom County into present-day Canada. The Lummi are also known as the Salmon People, a tribute to the sacrifice of Salmon Woman and the generations of Lummi fishermen and women who helped preserve that heritage.

It's a legacy that has been jeopardized by declining salmon runs in recent decades. The Salish Sea off the coast of Whatcom County was once thriving with multiple species of salmon, but the Lummi people have seen fewer fish returning to their upriver beds to spawn. It's a crisis that is being addressed at both the state and national level, but for the Lhaq'temish, it is yet another challenge they must rise to and overcome. Part of that effort lies within the tribe's Natural Resources Department, which operates the Lummi Bay Hatchery and the Skookum Creek Hatchery—facilities that rear and release millions of salmon annually. As part of their salmon enhancement efforts, tribal staff pump in both fresh and salt water from local sources.

The Lummi have been collaborating with the state's Department of Fish and Wildlife to help reverse the trend, but for the Salmon People, this mission is personal. It is a race to rescue their lifestyle and livelihood. Along with their shellfish operations and watershed restoration efforts, the Lummi remain remarkable stewards of the area's natural resources.

BLAINE HARBOR'S MARINE PARK

Just over twenty miles to the northwest of Bellingham lies the city of Blaine, an international border community with a long fishing and logging history. Blaine is known as the Gateway to the Pacific Northwest, and its most prominent monument is the sixty-seven-foot Peace Arch, dedicated in 1921 to commemorate the end of the War of 1812. The monument straddles the exact border between the United States and Canada and sees over half a million visitors annually.

Within sight of the Peace Arch monument is Blaine Marine Park, a quiet area where visitors can relax and both appreciate the natural beauty of the tidelands and ponder the significance of the area's industrial history. Reaching out into the water from the shoreline are rows of old pilings, on which several sawmills once stood a century ago; the mills' colorful remnants dot the beaches with flecks of red brick among the sand and rock. The park offers a nautical-themed playground and a few shelters for birdwatchers looking to spot numerous varieties of shorebirds and has several waterfront trails leading to the nearby marina.

Heading in that direction, visitors will pass the Blaine Harbor Boating Center on their way to the public fishing pier. The marina itself, now boasting over six hundred slips for commercial and pleasure boats, was once home to hundreds of commercial gillnetters and purse seiners operated by fishermen working the waters between Washington and Alaska.

Directly across from the fishing pier, explorers can see Tongue Point at the end of Semiahmoo (pronounced "SEM-ee-AH-moo") Spit, the other side of the entrance to Drayton Harbor. Semiahmoo Resort at the end of the spit is one of Washington's most popular destinations on account of its myriad luxury amenities and proximity to the water. Yet visitors today would hardly believe it was once the site of the largest salmon-canning operation in the world. In 1881, the first cannery was built at the end of Semiahmoo Spit, and 10 years later, it was purchased by the Alaska Packers

Remnants of once-vibrant waterfront industries are still visible at Blaine Marine Park, just south of the Peace Arch monument and the Canadian border. *Austin Stanley.*

Association (APA). Due to the sizeable output of the Alaskan salmon runs, the APA began expanding almost immediately and was operating thirty-one canneries in Alaska within its first 2 years. By the mid-1950s, the APA cannery in Blaine was packing one hundred thousand cases of salmon in a year, but the demand for canned salmon—and the seemingly endless supply—simply couldn't be sustained indefinitely. The APA merged with a few other food-packing companies and eventually began closing operations. It finally sold the Whatcom County cannery property in 1982, bringing an end to a 101-year-old industrial maritime operation.

To get to Semiahmoo from Blaine Harbor, explorers could make the twenty-minute trek around Drayton Harbor—but a simpler way would be to take the historic ferry, MV *Plover*, a unique and fun maritime experience. Tickets can be purchased at the Visitor Dock, Gate 2, at 235 Marine Drive in Blaine. The *Plover*, listed on the National Register of Historic Places, is owned by the City of Blaine and operated by the nonprofit Drayton Harbor Maritime. Built in 1944, the ferry can shuttle passengers (both two- and four-legged), along with strollers and bicycles, across to Tongue

Point, taking the same route on the same boat that cannery workers used to get to work in the 1940s. As a special treat, the *Plover*'s captain is known to let little ones pilot the ship for a spell, rewarding them with an honorary captain's certificate on arrival.

Once across the water, take the time to visit the Alaska Packers Association Cannery Museum at 9261 Semiahmoo Parkway. Housed in one of several original cannery buildings, the museum interprets the history of the APA using a scale-model fish trap, antique machinery, historical photos and an original twenty-nine-foot sailboat that once gillnetted salmon in Alaska. Admission is free.

Point Roberts History Center

Easily one of the most geographically unique and underappreciated areas of Washington, Point Roberts, for all intents and purposes, should really belong to Canada. Located just over twelve miles west of Blaine and surrounded on three sides by the Salish Sea, Point Roberts is only accessible from the United States by plane, boat or by vehicle traveling up into Canada, around Boundary Bay and back down again to the point. It's actually the end of the Canadian Tsawwassen Peninsula, a site historically used by myriad Indigenous tribes to fish for returning salmon. Now known as a pene-exclave of the United States, the nearly five square miles of Point Roberts boasts amazing natural views, an astounding assortment of marine life and numerous outdoor recreation opportunities.

Today's border between the United States and Canada came after a lengthy period of joint interest in the area by multiple countries, including the United States, Great Britain, Russia and Mexican California. The Treaty of 1818 narrowed joint occupation to just the United States and Great Britain, but tensions between the two countries festered until the Treaty of Oregon established today's international boundary at the forty-ninth parallel in 1846. The trouble is, the most accurate maps available at that time were drawn by George Vancouver and Charles Wilkes, neither of whom knew that the tiny point between Vancouver Island and the mainland fell *below* the forty-ninth parallel.

Thus, Point Roberts has remained U.S. soil ever since. While the issue of annexation or secession has surfaced periodically over the years, it hasn't gotten any traction from either country. For now, residents include a sizable number of Canadian citizens living across the border alongside American citizens who enjoy their congenial relationship with their northern neighbors. Point Roberts residents of both nationalities appreciate the area's maritime history.

Just over a decade after the Treaty of Oregon, the first permanent residents began to settle on the peninsula. Many were honest farmers and fishermen, but given its remote location and difficult accessibility, Point Roberts also attracted a host of lawless individuals looking to hide out from both countries' authorities. The United States soon purchased land to create a military reserve, but it never materialized, and the land was sold for development just over thirty years later. In 1893, the Alaska Packers Association bought a small cannery on the peninsula and built it into a major employer. Fishing operations soon sprang up to support the cannery, but the benefits to the small community were short-lived. The APA and other cannery owners had completely shut down operations by the time the state outlawed fish traps in the 1930s, effectively ending commercial fishing from Point Roberts. As the decades passed, the economic ebb and flow changed as often as the surrounding tides, but residents with a love for the Salish Sea have held fast to their pene-exclave throughout.

Point Roberts, Washington, was once an internationally advantageous site for maritime industries like salmon canning, as seen in this 1900s photo of the Alaska Packers Association Cannery. *Point Roberts Historical Society.*

Some of the best views and spectacular wildlife spotting take place at Point Roberts. Its southeastern corner, the Lily Point Marine Reserve, is the site of the former APA cannery and is arguably the most scenic spot on the peninsula. Tall clay cliffs overlook the vast stretches of salt water between the United States and Canada, and bald eagles are frequently seen circling above pods of orcas chasing salmon through the Strait of Georgia. Along the southern border, visitors will find the Point Roberts Marina and Resort, a haven for both United States and Canadian sailors and pleasure boaters. On the southwestern tip is Lighthouse Marine Park, a twenty-one-acre public space offering camping, beach access, picnic areas and more. One of the park's more interesting features is its inclusion in the Whale Trail, a series of sites along the North American Pacific coast from which to view marine mammals. There are over one hundred Whale Trail sites between California and British Columbia with interpretive signs to educate travelers about marine animal habitats, inspire stewardship of the vast but fragile ecosystem, connect visitors with each other and with the animals along the trail and protect marine resources for the benefit of current and future generations. To learn more and see a map of every site along the Whale Trail, visit www.thewhaletrail.org.

HUB CITY: ANACORTES

One of the more exotically named places in Skagit (SKADGE-it) County, the city of Anacortes is as scenic as it is hardy. Pronounced "ANN-uh-COR-tiss," this locale was named in the 1870s by the town's platter and promoter, Amos Bowman, who combined the first and maiden names of his wife, Anne Curtis. Anacortes is located at the northern point of Fidalgo Island within the traditional lands of the Samish people, who frequented the site for resource gathering, and non-Indigenous settlers begin residing there around the 1860s. Once it was on track to become the western terminus of a railroad expansion across the North Cascades to the Pacific, the town saw a frenzy of real estate and business interests scrambling to position themselves for the future.

However, shortly after the railroad's arrival, the town's biggest investment company went bankrupt and was unable to pay the thousands of workers installing a water system and wood-planked roads and building an electric trolley line. With an end to the jobs came a mass exodus of workers, and the town was forced to reinvent itself to survive. Hoping to turn the tide, the remaining residents began heavily promoting the area's improved infrastructure—which included four large ocean wharves—before finally incorporating in 1891.

All that promotion eventually caught the attention of a fishing magnate, who opted to locate his new cod-curing plant on the waterfront. His immediate success drew still other interests to the area, and the cod-packing industry soon expanded to include salmon and clam canning. By 1915, many of the largest canneries in the world lined the Anacortes waterfront, employing a diverse workforce made up of Japanese, Filipinos, Hawaiians, Puerto Ricans, Scandinavians, Croatians and others. Soon, the lumber and shipping industries began to flourish alongside Anacortes's canneries, and after two world wars, the oil industry established itself as well.

MARITIME HERITAGE CENTER AND THE *W.T. PRESTON*

With all this industry springing up in Anacortes, it became critical that goods could move freely from one place to another. Infrastructure as we know it didn't yet exist, so shippers relied on waterways to move their products to markets far and wide. That meant Anacortes needed both a robust shipping port with easy access to the Pacific as well as clear, navigable waterways to points inland.

At the Maritime Heritage Center in Anacortes, located at 703 R Avenue, visitors can experience the town's rich waterfront history through exhibits and artifacts related to Indigenous life in the area, early exploration, the fishing and cannery industries, shipbuilding, ferries and the Port of Anacortes's history, lumber mill operations and recreational boating in the twentieth century. Vintage movies and mural-size photographs from along the waterfront supplement the displays, along with the six-foot wooden wheel and telegraph from the historic ferry *Vashon*. The exhibits provide a complete overview of shoreline activities, including boatbuilding, mills and canneries, commercial and recreational boating, shipping and transportation.

Included in the exhibits is the story of Betty Lowman, who in 1937 rowed a dugout cedar canoe from Guemes Island across from Anacortes to Ketchikan, Alaska, a solo journey that spanned sixty-six days and over 1,300 miles through the treacherous Inside Passage. Lowman had received the canoe from her father as a gift after he found it adrift in 1931, and she named it *Bijaboji*, an acronym for the names of her four brothers: Bill, Jack, Bob and Jimmy. Over a quarter century after her momentous voyage, Lowman again rowed the *Bijaboji* back from Ketchikan to Anacortes, where the stalwart canoe remains on display at the Maritime Heritage Center.

Dominating the entryway to the center is the enormous sternwheel steamer *W.T. Preston*, one-third of a trio that once kept the area's inland

The U.S. Army Corps of Engineers is responsible for maintaining navigability on area rivers and harbors, once using steam-powered sternwheel snagboats such as the *W.T. Preston*, now on exhibit shoreside in Anacortes, Washington. *Public domain.*

waterways navigable. Now a National Historic Landmark, the *W.T. Preston*'s job from 1929 through 1981 was to remove navigational hazards from the bays and harbors of Puget Sound and the rivers feeding it. Fallen trees and other debris could create logjams, and shifting sand bars made river travel treacherous. The *W.T. Preston*—along with its predecessors, the *Skagit* (1885–1914) and the *Swinomish* (1914–29)—worked from Blaine to Olympia, clearing countless snags, logjams and other debris, including a damaged airplane and sunken marine vessels. Named for a distinguished civilian engineer who worked for the Army Corps of Engineers, the *W.T. Preston* was also used as a pile driver and an icebreaker and dredged about 3,500 cubic yards of material in an average year.

When the cost to maintain the *W.T. Preston* became prohibitive, the Army Corps of Engineers finally retired the storied steamer and sought for it a permanent home. The city of Anacortes was an excellent choice, given how much time the snagboat had spent in nearby waterways. In 1983, the *W.T. Preston* was hauled out of the water for the last time and moved to its current location, where it educates throngs of visitors annually about maritime history in Washington.

Admission to the Maritime Heritage Center is free, and guided tours of the snagboat cost five dollars. Note that admission must be paid in cash.

LA MERCED BREAKWATER

Heading west from downtown Anacortes, explorers may travel right past a sliver of history hidden cleverly from view. True to its origins, the city's northern waterfront remains engaged in maritime industry, as evidenced by the shipbuilding company Lovric's Sea-Craft. This nondescript blue-collar business along Guemes (pronounced "GWAY-mays") Channel includes a long pier, a small marina and a breakwater to protect them both from the tides. On closer inspection, however, visitors will see that the breakwater is actually the decaying hull of a once-proud four-masted schooner called *La Merced*.

Built in Benicia, California, in 1917, *La Merced*—whose name translates from Spanish to *The Mercy*—transported oil in barrels and boxes before being converted to a floating salmon cannery in 1926. At a time when it was costly and cumbersome to transport freshly caught fish to a land-based cannery, enterprising businessmen found ways to bring the cannery to the fishing grounds. One of those was a man named Nick Bez, a maritime mogul of the mid-twentieth century, who owned canneries from Alaska to Oregon. Bez, a Croatian whose real name was Nicoli Bezmalinovich, bought *La Merced* with the express purpose of streamlining the canning process to get his products to market faster. By the 1950s, the ship was churning out over sixty thousand cases of canned salmon annually, with nearly eight fishermen and crew aboard.

Then, in 1965, *La Merced* had seemingly reached the end of its useful life. Its owners sold the ship for scrap and had its engines, propellers, deck fittings, masts and bowsprit removed. Without any fanfare, *La Merced*'s naked hull was towed to the Lovric's site in 1966, strategically grounded and unceremoniously filled with dredged material from the marina. As the years passed, trees and bushes grew out of the dredged soil, further hiding the former schooner's identity.

La Merced's useful life, it turned out, was in fact extended, as it now provides Lovric's shipyard with an artificial refuge from the currents of the channel. Travelers are welcome to view the derelict hull from afar, but for

Built in 1917, *La Merced*—"The Mercy"—hauled petroleum before being converted to a floating fish cannery. After retirement, the schooner became a marina breakwater in Anacortes. *Ron Burke, Puget Sound Maritime Historical Society.*

safety reasons, the property owner has posted signs prohibiting exploration past the bow. At low tide, however, the best views of the ship can be accessed by walking the beach from nearby Roadside Park.

SHIP HARBOR INTERPRETIVE PRESERVE

Despite the decades of industrial expansion in Anacortes, residents also made the preservation of their environmental resources a high priority. The scenic waterfront bordered by lush green forests has long attracted visitors and new residents alike. Flanked by Cannery Lake to the west and the Ship Harbor Interpretive Preserve to the south, the Washington State Ferries terminal at the western end of town is known as the Gateway to the San Juans. The decaying pilings of long-gone canneries dot the waterfront of

Ship Harbor, so named after the USS *Massachusetts* anchored there to help protect American interests in the 1850s.

The preserve features a beautiful walking trail with numerous outlets for beach access. A walk there early in the morning will greet visitors with a cacophony of bird calls and, if conditions are right, a veil of mist blanketing the harbor. Numerous interpretive signs along the trail tell the story of the Samish people and their culture, the industrial development of Anacortes and the wildlife and natural wonders that can be found throughout the area. Perhaps most captivating to historical explorers are the algae-covered stone and brick cannery foundations nestled among the pilings, visible at low tide. Standing guard over this remnant of early twentieth-century industry are pelicans, cormorants, gulls and other seabirds sunning themselves or hopping from piling to piling as their whims dictate.

Whether visiting for the express purpose of seeing this unique mixture of nature and nautical heritage or whiling away time waiting for the next ferry to the San Juan Islands or Sidney, British Columbia, strolling the length of the Ship Harbor Interpretive Preserve is a maritime experience that should not be overlooked.

THE SWINOMISH TRIBE

On the southeast peninsula of Fidalgo Island lies the Swinomish Indian Reservation, a fifteen-square-mile homeland for its people. The Swinomish (anglicized from swədəbš and pronounced "SWIN-oh-mish") are known as the People of the Salmon and are descendants of those who signed the 1855 Treaty of Point Elliott. Prior to that, the Swinomish existed in bands living in longhouses and traveling around the area as resources became seasonally available. As with other Indigenous cultures in the Pacific Northwest, canoes were the primary means of transportation and greatly influenced the tribe's ability to defend itself and feed its people.

For thousands of years, the Swinomish fished for salmon, harvested shellfish, hunted wild game and gathered berries to survive. One of their primary routes of travel was the Swinomish Channel, but it didn't always look like it does today. The fabricated waterway was once a meandering slough, the depth of which fluctuated according to the tides. It brought resources to the Swinomish by flooding the flatlands twice a day, and the people built fish weirs to harvest returning salmon using the slough to reach

Members of the Swinomish Tribe historically traveled far in their canoes, as seen in this photo taken in the San Juan Islands about 1924. *Library of Congress.*

the north fork of the Skagit River. Within twenty-five years of the treaty, however, non-Indigenous efforts to make the slough more navigable for river traffic prompted the diking and dredging of the channel, forever changing the Swinomish way of life.

In 2008, the tribe began restoring marsh habitat along the Swinomish Channel with the goal of returning the waterway as much as possible to its original, natural condition. After removing a century's worth of dredged material from its banks, the tribe began seeing an increase in salmon spawning that indicated their efforts were bearing fruit. They began commercially growing and harvesting shellfish, and as time continues, the Swinomish people are eagerly anticipating the restoration of their aquacultural traditions. These expectations are brilliantly laid out in a series of interpretive panels along the Swinomish Channel on the reservation side. Visitors are invited to learn more about the history of the tribe and its culture by walking in the footsteps of their ancestors. Panels detailing the Swinomish way of life, their struggle to retain their identity after Euro-American incursion, the importance of canoes to their culture and much more help tell the tribe's story and share with visitors their perspective. A trio of shelters resembling cedar huts built along the waterway provide explorers with a place to rest, take in the views and imagine what the slough must have looked like to a generation of people who lived there centuries ago.

Rosario Beach and the Maiden of Deception Pass

Traveling down the western side of Fidalgo Island, explorers will notice Burrows Island across the bay. Accessible only by boat or aircraft, the island's westernmost point is home to the Burrows Island Lighthouse, a historic station built in 1906 and home to generations of lightkeeper families. Automated in 1973, the lighthouse was mostly left to the elements for over thirty years before volunteers from the Northwest Schooner Society committed to restoring the station in 2006. That work began in 2011 and has been mostly dependent on volunteer service and donations. At present, the lighthouse is closed to the public, but the society hopes that will change soon. In the meantime, independent visitors are warned that accessing the island is only possible via a partially submerged ladder that connects to a staircase leading up the steep cliffs to the boathouse. Until the lighthouse is fully restored and available for public use, enthusiasts are encouraged to make donations rather than in-person visits.

Continuing south, adventurers will reach Rosario Beach just before leaving Fidalgo Island via one of the most picturesque bridges to be found in western Washington. The views from the historic Canoe Pass and Deception Pass bridges are nothing short of spectacular, which is why travelers will often find them crowded with spectators parked on either end. If a spot opens, consider taking advantage and walking out onto the bridge. Or, for those afraid of heights, take the short path leading beneath the bridge for a more unique photo opportunity.

The Pacific Northwest Trail near Rosario Beach takes hikers through the oceanside forest around Bowman Bay, but Rosario Head itself offers something unique that any maritime traveler will appreciate. Rising from the neck of the peninsula is a large wooden sculpture of a woman holding a salmon above her head. From one side, she appears as a Native American dressed in traditional Samish garments. From the opposite side, her dress has become scales, her hair replaced by the bulbs and flowing strands of

The Samish Tribe's carved sculpture *Maiden of Deception Pass* has stood watch over Rosario Beach on Fidalgo Island since 1983. *Sean O'Neill.*

kelp adorned with fish and shells. The carving is of Ko-kwal-alwoot (also spelled Kwuh-kwal-uhl-wut, anglicized from Kʷəkʷáləlwət), the Maiden of Deception Pass, and her legend comes from the Samish Indian Nation, anglicized from S7ámesh and known as "the people who stand up and give." Generations of Samish have lived on Fidalgo, Guemes and other islands around the area for thousands of years, all the while developing their intimate connection with the sea.

As the story goes, Ko-kwal-alwoot was gathering food from the beach when a shellfish slipped from her fingers. She reached into the water to grab it and it slipped again. Over and over this happened, bringing her deeper into the sea. When she reached in a final time, she felt a hand from beneath the surface grasp hers. Scared as she was, a voice told her not to be afraid and that her captor simply wanted to gaze on her beauty for a while. When she was released, she returned to her people, but she came back to the sea repeatedly to meet with the spirit who held her hand. Each time, she remained a little longer while the spirit told her of the many beautiful things within the waves.

One day, a young man came forth from the ocean and asked to meet with Ko-kwal-alwoot's father. She brought him home, where he asked her father for her hand in marriage. Startled, her father refused, saying that she would die if she went with him beneath the waves. But the man insisted that she would not die but live forever among the beauty of the ocean because he loved her so much. Then, he offered her father a warning: if he did not acquiesce and release Ko-kwal-alwoot to be his bride, all the people's food would be taken from them. The streams would dry up, and the ocean would no longer provide its bounty. Still, her father refused, and the man returned to his ocean home without a wife.

Very soon after, his foretelling became a reality. The people began to starve, and they had no water to drink because the streams had disappeared. Finally, when she could no longer bear to see her people suffering, Ko-kwal-alwoot went back to the sea to find the man and beg him to feed her people. He gave her a message for her father: only when she agreed to marry him would the fish return with the water and the people again live in abundance. Ko-kwal-alwoot's father reluctantly agreed, with one enduring request— that she be allowed to return to her people once a year, so they knew she was happy and well cared for.

Ko-kwal-alwoot did return to her people, and the food supply returned, more plentiful than before. Yet, each year, when she emerged from the water, the people noticed she was changing. Barnacles began growing on her hands, and scales on her dress, and the last time she visited her people, they noticed that she was unhappy out of the sea. They told her they loved her but she belonged with her husband and did not need to return to them again unless it was her wish to do so. One last time, she walked deeper into the water until all that could be seen of her was her hair floating on the surface.

Today, when members of the Samish Indian Nation see the kelp beds flowing back and forth with the currents, they believe that Ko-kwal-alwoot is there, her hair drifting gently with the tide as she forever watches out for the welfare of her people.

HUB CITY: COUPEVILLE

Once across the bridges of Deception Pass, explorers will find themselves on Whidbey Island, a magnificent getaway destination loaded with as much history as it has scenic beauty. Along with Camano Island, its smaller sibling to the east, the pair comprise all of Island County. Once used by several Indigenous tribes for fishing, hunting and gathering, the island was named after Royal Navy officer Joseph Whidbey by George Vancouver in 1792. By the time Charles Wilkes arrived nearly fifty years later, the island's Native population had been joined by a Catholic mission.

The first non-Indigenous settler on Whidbey Island was Isaac Ebey (pronounced "EE-bee"), who moved his family from Olympia to homestead the island in 1850. Looking to establish a presence, the Ebey family spread out and began farming the rich soil on Whidbey Island. Ebey made use of the naturally forgiving beachfront along his property and built a dock to receive commercial shipments from nearby Port Townsend. After a few years, tensions between area tribes and settlers began to increase, so Ebey and his family constructed several blockhouses to provide protection in case of Indian attack. Some of those blockhouses can still be visited on the island today.

Whidbey Island is home to a naval air station on the north side near the city of Oak Harbor, and island residents are accustomed to hearing the roar of jets flying overhead from time to time. For just five dollars, explorers interested in the aviation aspect of naval activities can visit the Pacific Northwest Naval Air Museum in Oak Harbor Wednesdays through Sundays before five o'clock.

There are two ferry terminals on Whidbey Island, one to the west taking travelers across Admiralty Inlet to Port Townsend and the other to the east in Clinton, linking islanders with Mukilteo back on the mainland. Near the island's middle is the city of Coupeville (pronounced "COOP-vill"), the Island County seat, named after Captain Thomas Coupe, who laid out the town in the 1850s. Fort Ebey State Park lies just outside of Coupeville, as does Ebey's Landing National Historical Reserve—the first such reserve in the country.

Historic Coupeville Wharf

At the northernmost point of downtown Coupeville lies its most iconic structure, though it isn't the first of its kind. The historic 1905 wharf at the foot of Alexander Street on Penn Cove is an excellent example of how historic structures can be revitalized by finding a new purpose for them.

In the mid- to late 1800s, Coupeville had numerous wharves and docks along the cove, some only accessible at high tide, which helped islanders receive goods from the mainland. The island's population increased after completion of nearby Fort Casey in 1901, so local farmers and merchants banded together to build the current wharf five hundred feet out into the water. The great length of the wharf was necessary to compensate for tidal changes and accommodate steamboat traffic that regularly picked up and dropped off passengers at Coupeville. In 1909, a man named Elmer Calhoun purchased the wharf and made several improvements to it over the years. Adding a grain tower and restrooms that "flushed" with the tide, Calhoun remodeled the wharf in the 1930s, ensuring it would remain an active part of the Coupeville community for the foreseeable future.

When engineers completed the bridges at Deception Pass in 1936, it effectively ended steamship travel to the island via the Coupeville Wharf. Calhoun sold the wharf in 1949 to the Coupeville Wharf and Seed Company, which continued renovations for the next several decades. Though merchants continued to use the wharf to move products on and off the island, it was clear by the 1980s that the structure had outlived its original purpose. But within a decade, owners had begun converting the wharf—which had once greeted thousands of steamship passengers during the town's seafaring days—into retail and commercial space.

Coupeville travelers may find street parking a bit sparse, especially on warm summer days and weekends, so be prepared to walk from the

The 1925 wooden schooner *Suva* offers classic sailing experiences from the 1905 Coupeville Historic Wharf, still an iconic part of the area's vibrant waterfront community. *Port of Coupeville.*

public parking lot a few blocks to the south. On the way, visitors will pass by the Island County Historical Museum, featuring exhibits, artifacts and interpretive panels about early residents of the island. The museum is housed in an elegant building with a lovely wraparound porch, an abstract recreation of another building that once stood on that spot; the 1868 Blockhouse Inn, so named for its proximity to the Alexander Blockhouse (which still stands today), burned to the ground in its centennial anniversary year. There are several examples of traditional Salish canoes on display in front of the museum, and across the street is the museum's former home from 1971 through 1991. Originally the town's 1937 firehouse, the building now houses the Coupeville Chamber of Commerce and visitor center.

Continuing to the historic Coupeville wharf, explorers will find a coffee shop, gift store, modern restrooms, a restaurant and boat moorage. Hanging in the building's foyer is the reconstructed skeleton of a thirty-three-foot gray whale named Rosie, and adventurers can charter whale-watching trips or rent kayaks at the facility.

Langley Whale Center

Heritage-minded visitors to Whidbey will be pleased to know there are multiple history museums scattered across the thin and winding island. On the south end, in the town of Langley, is another experience waiting for maritime enthusiasts to discover. The Langley Whale Center is operated by the Orca Network, a nonprofit organization connecting whales and people in the Pacific Northwest for nearly thirty years. Staffed by resolute environmentalists and animal activists, the Orca Network exists to help educate the public about Salish Sea whales, track sightings of the magnificent creatures, provide news and information about them in the form of programs and commentary and generally advocate for the welfare of marine mammals.

The Langley Whale Center at 105 Anthes Avenue is ground zero for those efforts, offering visitors both a gift shop experience as well as the chance to be a scientist-activist by participating in whale-sighting or captive orca release projects. Together with the Central Puget Sound Marine Mammal Stranding Network—which assists stranded animals, collects data and specimens for research and provides public education about marine mammals—the Whale Center is home to a small army of passionate volunteers dedicated to celebrating and sharing the stories of endangered southern resident orcas and north Puget Sound gray whales that feed in the waters of Saratoga Passage and Possession Sound each March through May.

The center is filled with both art and artifacts relating to marine mammals, including enormous skulls, fins and vertebrae on display, several educational videos for both kids and adults, whale identification posters, an ocean listening experience, a real-time whale-sighting map, books and materials about the study of whales and other creatures of the deep and more. Visitors will find staff at the Langley Whale Center always ready for a lively conversation about their finned friends. Admission is free, donations are welcome and memberships to help support the cause are always appreciated.

One block north of the Langley Whale Center at the foot of Anthes Avenue is the colorful entrance to Seawall Park. The park is known locally as one of the best places to view feeding gray whales from land, and its entrance is flanked on one side by a mural featuring a pair of rainbow wings intended for selfie-taking and an antique metal-and-glass structure once known as a phone booth before the word "selfie" was ever coined. A few steps into the park, visitors will find a sculpture of Hope the Wishing Whale, which invites contributors to drop a donation into the whale's blowhole to support arts and public spaces in Langley. Next to the sculpture is a small station encouraging viewers to ring a bell when whales are spotted from the park. A few more steps toward the water and whale watchers can step onto a small platform with a railing, benches, an interpretive panel and a free telescope with which they can scan the waters for whale spouts. At the bottom of the hill, visitors will find Langley's seawall park, with public access to Saratoga Passage. There are also numerous options for dining, drinking and shopping to be found in town after exploring the seawall.

South Whidbey Historical Museum

One of the dining options in Langley is called Spyhop, named after the curious behavior of orcas poking their heads above water to look around. The cozy neighborhood pub is located just a block southwest of the Langley Whale Center and directly across Second Street from the South Whidbey Historical Museum. Visitors will find it packed with interesting information, artifacts, photographs and more—all related to the history of the southern half of Whidbey Island. Given that access to the island was exclusively ship-based for so long, many of the stories told at the museum are maritime-related. For example, one of the most striking tales is the sinking of the Mosquito Fleet vessel *Calista* on July 28, 1922. Under a thick blanket of fog, Captain Bert Lovejoy disembarked from Langley in the late morning, having already made several stops around Puget Sound. Shortly before eleven o'clock, hearing blasts from ships' horns but unable to locate them through the dense atmosphere, Captain Lovejoy stopped the ship off West Point just north of Seattle and tried to get his bearings by listening. Without warning, the 9,482-ton Japanese steam freighter *Hawaii Maru* appeared off the port bow and rammed the 105-ton *Calista* at full speed.

The captain of the *Hawaii Maru* is credited with helping prevent the *Calista* from immediately sinking to the bottom of Elliott Bay by ordering his ship to continue ahead at one-quarter speed, pinning the *Calista* to its bow. The extra time gave passengers a chance to either board lifeboats or jump ship and swim to rescue aboard the freighter or nearby tugs that came to aid in the recovery effort. By the time the *Calista*'s forward flagpole finally slipped beneath the surface twenty-eight minutes later, all seventy passengers and crew members had been rescued. The *Seattle Post-Intelligencer* reported the following day that, other than the mayor of Langley fainting, no passenger suffered so much as wet feet in the marine disaster.

The *Hawaii Maru* later served as a Japanese troop transport during World War II and was torpedoed and sunk by the submarine USS *Sea Devil* in the East China Sea. What happened to the wreckage of the *Calista* can be discovered at the South Whidbey Historical Museum, 312 Second Street in Langley.

Ebey's Landing

Isaac Ebey and his family were some of the first non-Indigenous people to permanently settle on Whidbey Island, and their land claim comprised a large amount of territory and beachfront just south of where Coupeville is today. Along the middle of the island's western coastline is an expansive amount of farmland overlooking relatively calm waters at the entrance to Admiralty Inlet, bifurcated by long, undulating bluffs offering visitors spectacular views.

Gazing across the broad, sweeping beaches on Whidbey Island's western shores, it's easy to see what drew both explorers and homesteaders to this location. *Washington Our Home.*

It is along these beaches that the Ebeys constructed a dock to help facilitate commerce and move the grains and produce grown on the farms. Isaac Ebey became an outspoken promoter of a ferry system, helping to create the first regular runs from Port Townsend to Whidbey Island, and his landing found usage through the beginning of the twentieth century.

There are numerous stories told at the Ebey's Landing National Historical Reserve, established in 1978 to protect the natural beauty of the area and interpret its history. Explorers of the island today will find farms, fields, roads, structures and natural features that are all remnants of the island's early settlement and development. Visitors can stroll the long, windswept beaches, ascend the oceanside cliffs to take in the view or meander through the farmland, marveling at its agricultural richness.

Between Memorial Day and Labor Day, visitors to this National Historical Reserve can stop at the Jacob and Sarah Ebey House Visitor Center, the original home of Isaac's parents, who traveled across the Oregon Trail along with their daughters, Mary and Ruth, and their son Winfield to live near their son Isaac. Volunteer docents should be available with maps, trail guides and visitor information, and the quarter-mile path to the center is lined with interpretive panels. There are campgrounds nearby, as well as hiking trails and other opportunities for exploration within the reserve, so adventurers will want to spend some time in the area.

Fort Casey and Admiralty Head Lighthouse

Visitors to Whidbey Island usually depart via the Deception Pass bridges to the north, the eastside ferry terminal at Clinton or the westside ferry terminal directly south of Coupeville. That ferry dock is located just outside Fort Casey, one-third of what once comprised the "Triangle of Fire" guarding the entrance to Puget Sound. Built in the late 1800s, Fort Casey—along with Fort Worden near Port Townsend and Fort Flagler on Marrowstone Island across Admiralty Inlet—was used as a coastal defense and training facility until after World War II, when all three properties were absorbed into the Washington State Parks inventory.

Fort Casey, like its counterparts across the water, came about after the United States saw a significant advancement in military technology between the Civil War and the Spanish-American War thirty years later. It became clear to officials in Washington, D.C., that American coastlines needed an improved defense network to prevent incursions by enemy speedboats, gunships and submarines. Then-president Grover Cleveland appointed a joint army, navy and civilian board to study options, headed by Secretary of War William C. Endicott and known as the Board of Fortifications or, more commonly, the Endicott Board.

By the time Fort Casey was activated in 1901, it featured ten-inch "disappearing" guns that could be loaded beneath the bunker wall, raised up to aim and fire and returned to a safe, unseen position. These massive guns were often fired for training purposes during the lifespan of the fort; however, they were never used in actual defense. The invention of military aircraft soon rendered the forts created by the Endicott Board vulnerable from above, and subsequent world wars eventually negated any tactical usefulness they served. Fort Casey saw use as a military training ground for a time, but by the mid-1950s, there were no valid reasons to keep the installation active. It became a state park in 1955, and in the decades since, it has become one of the most popular destinations for heritage tourism in Washington.

Among the historical attractions at Fort Casey State Park are massive, ten-inch "disappearing" guns installed in the early 1900s and designed to protect defense production and military facilities in the Puget Sound area. *Washington State Parks*.

Exploring Fort Casey today will not leave visitors unimpressed. Fort Casey Historical State Park is a 999-acre marine area featuring numerous camping options and nearly two miles of saltwater shoreline. Kids and military history buffs alike will marvel at the pair of ten-inch disappearing guns still mounted in their emplacements, as well as two additional three-inch mounted guns on display. The fort has an interpretive center with a gift shop, as well as miles of unnerving subterranean passageways connecting old ammunition storage rooms with troop barracks, strategy rooms and gun batteries. Along with its sibling forts across the inlet, Fort Casey is one of the most interesting and unique places for a maritime or military enthusiast to explore in Washington today.

And for visitors who prefer a more romantic getaway destination, Fort Casey is home to one of the more picturesque lighthouses to be found around the state. The 1902 Admiralty Head Lighthouse is a two-story building of Italianate Revival design and includes a residence for the lightkeeper. Navigational use of Admiralty Head Lighthouse discontinued in 1922, and Washington State Parks assumed ownership along with Fort Casey in the 1950s. Partnering with a nonprofit organization called the Lighthouse Environmental Program, the state meticulously restored the magnificent structure to its former glory (including the lantern house, which had been transferred to the New Dungeness Lighthouse in 1927).

Dedicated volunteers of the Lighthouse Environmental Program provide tours, rotating exhibits and events; display artifacts; and continue to research the lighthouse's history at the site today. Maritime travelers would be remiss to overlook a visit to Admiralty Head Lighthouse when exploring the batteries of Fort Casey on Whidbey Island.

HUB CITY: FRIDAY HARBOR

The San Juan Islands in the north Salish Sea possess some of the most unique and picturesque locations in all of Washington. Made up of San Juan, Orcas, Lopez, Shaw, Blakely, Decatur and a few smaller islands, San Juan County is as historic as it is beautiful. The islands can be reached via ferries connecting Friday Harbor on San Juan Island with Sidney, British Columbia (Canada), Port Townsend along Washington's Olympic Peninsula or Anacortes in Skagit County to the east.

Spanish explorer Francisco de Eliza named the islands when he charted them in 1791. Friday Harbor is named in honor of Joseph Poalie Friday, a native Hawaiian who raised sheep around the harbor in the 1860s. It is the most populous town in the islands, giving off a busy but not crowded feel. This cute seaside village features clean, terraced streets lined with nautical-themed boutique shops, restaurants, quaint hotels, coffeehouses, gardens and gift shops (as well as several realty businesses trying to entice vacationers to become permanent residents). Visitors to the island could easily spend an entire weekend exploring just what Friday Harbor has to offer, but since there is so much history on San Juan Island, it would be a shame not to venture out.

One of the first stops travelers will appreciate is the Whale Museum, an institution with as many educational tidbits about marine mammals as souvenirs available in the gift shop. Opened in 1979 as the first museum in America devoted to a living animal species, the Whale Museum helps promote stewardship of the Salish Sea ecosystem through education and research. Visitors can take advantage of two floors filled with exhibits, maps, movies and more. Guests who've ever wondered why some whales have teeth while others have baleen can find answers here. Beachcombers having difficulty telling pinnipeds apart can learn about the distinguishing features of both seals and sea lions. One of the most interesting features of the museum is the depth of research into the lineage of the endangered Southern Resident orcas. This community of killer whales is composed of three family groups, called pods, with as many as four generations traveling together. Named the J, K and L pods, they have around seventy-five whales between them, and marine enthusiasts can sift through pictures of each member, learn their names and identifying marks, discover which are related to each other (and how) and find out why Southern Resident orcas eat salmon while other killer whales hunt seals and sea lions. It's a fascinating dive into the ancestry and appetites of odontocetes and absolutely worth the price of admission.

There are several interesting lighthouses scattered across the islands, as well. The 1935 Cattle Point Lighthouse stands as a solitary beacon among the rolling southern plains of San Juan Island, while the Turn Point Lighthouse on nearby Stuart Island illuminates the marine border between the United States and Canada. On the western side of the northernmost island is the Patos Island Lighthouse, another storied building that serves as a breathtaking photographic focal point. If they find the right angle (usually by boat), maritime explorers can capture a sunrise over a distant Mount Baker with the lighthouse atop the rocky edge of the island surrounded by the Salish Sea. It would be hard to find a photo more representative of the beauty of western Washington unless an orca were to surface at that exact moment—which is a very real possibility.

San Juan Island National Historical Park

The second largest of the islands in the archipelago, San Juan is brimming with not just state but world history. There are two places on the island that tell the story of the Pig War, otherwise known as the Bloodless War, the War That Wasn't or the San Juan Boundary Dispute of 1859. Both places are part of San Juan Island National Historical Park; the northernmost is known as English Camp and the southernmost as American Camp.

The Hudson's Bay Company (HBC), a British fur and mercantile trading outfit established in 1670, had been grazing sheep on San Juan Island for six years before the international incident and had laid claim to the island as early as 1845. The Americans—having declared Washington a U.S. territory in 1853—began ardently homesteading it as unsuccessful prospectors steadily returned to the area after the California gold rush. One such homesteader, Lyman Cutlar, disgruntled about HBC pigs once again knocking down his fence and uprooting his potatoes, grabbed his gun and chased after the offending swine. When the pig stopped at the edge of the forest, Cutlar shouldered his rifle and shot it dead.

Numerous books have been written about what happened next, some focusing on the reckless escalation of naval and military firepower and others on the involvement of some famous (and infamous) historical names: George Pickett, Winfield Scott and Kaiser Wilhelm the First, to name a few. Maritime explorers, however, may be most interested in a few specific aspects of the Pig War, a fortunately bloodless conflict that pitted the United States against Great Britain for the third time in less than eighty years.

At the American Camp Visitor Center, 4668 Cattle Point Road, travelers can take a history walk through the restored remains of the American military camp to a place called Robert's Redoubt, an earthen battlement designed and built by Second Lieutenant Henry Robert to provide the Americans with a mostly uninterrupted 260-degree view of the Salish Sea. This allowed U.S. forces to observe any approaching British warships, such as the HMS *Tribune*, the HMS *Satellite* and the HMS *Plumper*. Another trail leading directly south from the visitor center takes hikers through the site of the former HBC operation, known as the Belle Vue Sheep Farm, to explore the windswept seaside cliffs. All that remains of the farm today is a solitary flagpole in the middle of a field and dozens of footpaths etched into the terrain by flocks of sheep over a century and a half ago.

Fifteen miles across the island at what is now the English Camp Visitor Center, 3905 West Valley Road, Royal Marines trained daily for a potential war with the United States over the misguided murder of a wayward hog. Visitors can hike down to the parade grounds, tour the restored buildings, meander through the formal garden, gaze at the tranquility of Garrison Bay and see something rarely witnessed in America today: representatives of the federal government raising or lowering the British flag over American soil. Seven soldiers who perished from various accidents during the occupation are buried on a quiet hillside southwest of the English

American Camp as it looked about 1868, after nearly a decade of joint occupation by British and American forces. *Public domain.*

The HMS *Boxer* is depicted here moored to the pier at English Camp on San Juan Island sometime in the 1860s. *Public domain.*

Camp Visitor Center. A trail leads hikers across West Valley Road and up to the cemetery, where the graves are surrounded by a white picket fence as well as interpretive signage about their occupants and how they died.

For twelve years, the American and British governments negotiated to find a peaceful resolution to the standoff. Between 1860 and 1872, Canada became its own country, the U.S. Civil War began and ended and the men of two countries stationed on San Juan Island learned to live with each other, often celebrating each other's national holidays and engaging in good-natured sporting competitions. By the time Germany's Kaiser Wilhelm the First appointed a three-man commission to arbitrate the dispute in 1872 (eventually deciding in favor of the Americans), both countries had moved on to more pressing issues. With little fanfare, the Royal Marines departed San Juan Island, bringing an end to the so-called Pig War without so much as a single casualty—save, of course, for the pig.

LIME KILN POINT STATE PARK

There is more to the man who unwittingly ignited the Pig War with his impulsive shot. Lyman Cutlar wasn't just a failed prospector turned potato farmer. In 1860, Cutlar and others began commercially mining limestone on San Juan Island. Created by the accumulation of organic material such as shells and coral, limestone can be heated to extreme temperatures and turned into lime, which is vital to agricultural and industrial processes like the manufacture of cement, steel, glass and soil additives.

Visitors to Lime Kiln Point State Park on the island's western shore can explore the Lime Kiln Lighthouse. Yet another of Washington's picturesque navigational aids, the 1918 structure has helped protect mariners from the rocky point on which it stands for over a century. Easily one of the most photographed lighthouses in the state due to the Olympic Mountains providing a dramatic backdrop, the Lime Kiln Lighthouse was deemed a state and national historic site in 1978 and has delighted visitors to San Juan Island ever since.

In the 1980s, the Whale Museum in Friday Harbor began using the lighthouse as a research station. Due to the frequent presence of orcas off the point, scientists installed underwater cameras and a microphone (called a hydrophone) to watch and listen to passing cetaceans. Just outside the lighthouse is an orca-listening station, where whale watchers can hear

Built in 1918, Lime Kiln was the last lighthouse in Washington to be electrified, not receiving this technological upgrade until the Bonneville Power Administration laid a submarine power cable from Anacortes to the San Juan Islands in 1951. *Washington Our Home.*

the sounds made by the marine mammals they spot from shore. There is such a variety of maritime and heritage-related activities at Lime Kiln Point State Park that any adventurer exploring San Juan Island should consider it a top priority.

ROCHE HARBOR

One of the industrialists who capitalized on the area's rich limestone deposits was a man named John Stafford McMillin, founder of the Tacoma and Roche Harbor Lime Company. In 1886, McMillin—a Tacoma lawyer who discovered the rich deposit of limestone at the site—began construction of his business at Roche (pronounced "ROACH") Harbor. It included multiple lime kilns (like those found at Lime Kiln Point State Park), as well as a lime production factory, barrel manufacturer, warehouse, company store, churches, homes, piers, a fleet of ships and even a hotel. In one place, McMillin could mine, process, store, pack and ship his product, as well as access a labor force with places to live and shop. Roche Harbor had become a true company town, and many of its residents were Japanese immigrants who helped increase the company's output from 8,000 to 150,000 barrels a year.

McMillin built his twenty-room hotel around the remnants of a Hudson's Bay Company trading post, part of which can still be viewed today. Dubbed Hotel de Haro (after a 1787 sailing expedition led by Captain Gonzalo López de Haro, who also lends his name to nearby Haro Strait), the opulent accommodations once provided rest and relaxation for President Theodore Roosevelt. The hotel was originally used as temporary employee housing and later as the McMillan family residence while their home was being finished, but visitors to Roche Harbor today will be in awe of how pristine the hotel has been kept throughout years. Though the rooms now number nineteen, and many of them share bathrooms, the experience of sleeping in such a historic environment has entranced

Guests of the historic Hotel de Haro have gazed across the placid waters of San Juan Island's Roche Harbor since 1886. *Roche Harbor Resort.*

maritime enthusiasts since the hotel was converted to a resort destination in 1956. Along with Quarryman Hall, McMillin Suites (formerly the family's home), Village Homes, Historic Cottages and Condominiums, the Roche Harbor Resort at 248 Reuben Memorial Drive has something for every travel style and budget.

If land-based accommodations aren't preferred, the marina at Roche Harbor Resort is arguably one of the best in Washington. The professional marina team welcomes boaters of all types, and mariners can take full advantage of everything the resort offers. Connecting the marina with the mainland is the former company store, a historic building now housing a grocer, gift shop, post office, restrooms with showers, laundry facilities and the Lime Kiln Café. For the extra adventurous, there are even floatplane excursions available from the marina.

For explorers who find the history of the island fascinating and want to learn more, consider visiting the San Juan Historical Museum at 405 Price Street in Friday Harbor. It holds a wealth of information about the island and its early residents, including its Coast Salish history, the McMillin family, their Japanese employees and more.

Orcas Island

The largest of the county's islands (by 2.25 square miles over San Juan), Orcas Island is surprisingly not named after the killer whales so frequently seen in the surrounding waters. Like many of its sister islands, Orcas was named by Spanish explorer Francisco de Eliza in 1791 after the viceroy of New Spain who sponsored Eliza's expedition, Juan Vicente de Güemes Padilla Horcasitas y Aguayo, Second Count of Revillagigedo. Orcas Island is a shortened version of the name Horcasitas. Despite the misleading moniker, visitors are never far from stunning ocean views and miles of beaches to explore. Explorers can stop by the Orcas Island Historical Museum at 181 North Beach Road in Eastsound to learn more about the island's history or find several scenic hiking trails to get closer to nature.

While looking for good hikes on Orcas Island, it would be a shame to miss one that leads to the most impressive and expansive view in the San Juans. Orcas Island is home to Moran State Park, a 5,400-acre wonderland of forests; freshwater lakes; hiking, biking and equestrian trails; and more. Moran State Park is named after Robert Moran, a pivotal figure in Seattle's

First constructed around 1905 as the Orcas Island home of noted Seattle shipbuilder and onetime city mayor Robert Moran, the renovated Rosario Resort has welcomed guests since its opening in 1960. *National Park Service*.

maritime history. After arriving in the Pacific Northwest from New York in 1875, Moran soon began building and repairing ships with his brothers at Yesler's Wharf. As his wealth and social stature grew, his political ambitions followed shortly thereafter, and citizens elected Moran mayor of Seattle in 1888. When the Great Seattle Fire of 1889 destroyed his business (along with twenty-five city blocks, including the entire business district), Moran set to work rebuilding. By the time the Klondike gold rush arrived in the mid-1890s, the Moran Brothers Company had positioned itself to provide a fleet of paddleboats to miners on the Yukon River. Its success led to additional shipbuilding contracts, culminating in the launch of the USS *Nebraska*, Washington's only battleship, in 1904.

The following year, forty-seven-year-old Moran received distressing news. His doctors predicted his early death from heart disease within a year, so Moran left his shipbuilding business and moved to a sprawling estate on Orcas Island, where he designed and built a five-level, fifty-four-room mansion. Named Rosario after the strait between the San Juan Islands and the mainland, it served as the Moran family home until they sold it in 1938, and Robert died five years later at age eighty-six—nearly four decades after his terminal diagnosis.

The Rosario Resort and Spa, as it's known today, still stands majestically overlooking the placid waters of East Sound. Featuring some of the finest materials Moran could import, the artsy design of Rosario also included a nod to the nautical, as some of the bedrooms feature ship's bunks, there's a figurehead from a clipper ship in the resort's garden and the chain surrounding the property once held the anchor of the USS *Nebraska* itself. Moran also dammed a nearby lake to supply electricity to the mansion, which it still does today. Visitors to Rosario can browse through original photographs from the era as well as an extensive display of the ships built by Moran Brothers Company. Best of all for maritime explorers, the Rosario Resort includes a thirty-slip marina and a museum dedicated to the shipbuilding tycoon and his storied, unexpectedly long life.

LOPEZ ISLAND

Those looking for a more private maritime heritage experience may consider traveling to Lopez Island, the least developed of the commercial islands in the chain. It is named after Spanish explorer Gonzalo López de Haro (Haro Strait, Hotel de Haro), who sailed in the 1790–91 expedition commanded by Francisco de Eliza. After disembarking at the ferry landing at the island's northern tip, visitors will want to travel the four and a half miles south to the Lopez Island Historical Museum, which features a near–fully restored gillnetter named the *Sally J* in its parking lot—near–fully restored because a portion of the port side hull has been left untouched behind plexiglass, giving visitors a glimpse between the aging ribs and into the inner workings of the ship. Gillnetting is a fishing technique first used by Native Americans who frequented the islands, in which natural fiber nets would have stones attached to the bottom and wooden floats attached to the top. In 1930, the *Sally J* employed a similar technique using more modern apparatuses, fishing the waters off Lopez Island for over fifty years. Using linen nets and buoys, two crew members would haul in the catch from the stern before returning to one of the island's fisheries. Prior to the invention of monofilament, fish could see the linen netting in the daylight, so crews would set out to ply the waters from dusk until dawn, often getting only a few hours' sleep before having to prepare for the next evening's run.

At the Lopez Island Historical Museum, visitors can view one section of the restored gillnetter *Sally J* that has been left in original condition. *Washington Our Home.*

Maritime enthusiasts will enjoy a trip through the free museum at 28 Washburn Place. The grounds are dotted with gardens, historic farming equipment and relics from nautical vessels that either helped feed islanders or transported them to and from their homes. Inside, visitors will find photographs, interpretive panels and models of historic ships that once represented a lifeline to Lopezians (locals pronounce it "low-PEE-shuns") from long ago. The steamer *Rosalie* is featured prominently, as is the *Harvester King*, a kelp-collecting ship that was reconfigured to provide vehicle ferry service in 1922.

Travelers interested in a more intimate maritime experience might want to hike out to Iceberg Point at the island's southernmost tip. In addition to the breathtaking views of the water from high atop weatherworn cliffs, explorers will also discover the Treaty of 1908 marker, one of several scattered across the San Juans. The trail to Iceberg Point cuts through private property, but neighbors have consented to allow access provided hikers are quiet and keep the route clean.

The short hike through a wooded area gives way to a rocky outcropping, on which sits a concrete obelisk commemorating the border agreement between the United States and the United Kingdom's Dominion of Canada. Signed on April 11, 1908, the treaty called for expert surveyors to determine the exact maritime border between the two countries for the purposes of ending fishing disputes, among other things. This particular monument to international cooperation is known as Turning Point 7 and indicates exactly how far from the marker the border is (17,053.4 meters N 88° 46' 49" W, for those who go looking).

PART III

SOUTH
PUGET SOUND

Pierce, Thurston
and Mason Counties

HUB CITY: TACOMA

Rich in state and maritime history, Tacoma has a vibrant, storied past that has contributed to the city's endearing, often eccentric nature. First settled by non-Indigenous residents in the early 1850s, it wasn't until 1873, when the Northern Pacific Railroad selected a site south of the river delta as the western terminus of its cross-country line, that Tacoma began firmly establishing itself in Washington. In 1880, there were barely one thousand people living in the new community, but within a decade it had swelled to over thirty-six thousand. The Northern Pacific constructed a magnificent building to house its western operation—a historic structure in downtown that serves today as a federal courthouse—and merchants built wharves on the tideflats to connect the new railroad with shipping opportunities. Soon, a streetcar line branched out from the heart of the city to connect neighboring communities, and Tacoma had come of age as a thriving city rivaling Seattle to the north.

Some of the first maritime trade Tacoma saw came from Asia, as tea companies began using Tacoma as their port of call instead of San Francisco. Soon, additional ships started arriving with rice, silk and other goods, and the tideflats began to develop into an industrial area. Beyond the flats, the Tacoma waterfront kept pace, lining Commencement Bay with warehouses, passenger docks and other maritime-related businesses. Then, in 1918, a public vote officially created the Port of Tacoma, which began formally shipping goods in 1921. The first cargo was a load of lumber, and workers set a world record by loading the six hundred thousand board feet aboard a ship in less than twenty-four hours.

Tacoma has long depended on its working waterfront, as shown in this 1915 image of two Mosquito Fleet passenger steamers and the U.S. Army transport *Burnside* moored to the Tacoma Municipal Dock. *Tacoma Public Library General Photograph Collection TPL-1913.*

As the port continued to grow and more goods made their way in and out of Tacoma, the need for storage of those goods increased. Soon, there was an extensive line of warehouses on the city's waterfront, some of which were stacked floor to ceiling with grain bags and other cargo. Tacoma's municipal dock, the first in the state when it opened in 1911, became crowded with ships of all types, from ocean liners and Mosquito Fleet ferries to military ships and privately owned pleasure craft.

Visitors to the Port of Tacoma today may have a challenging time finding their way around. The tideflats are a noisy maze of streets, cargo warehouses, businesses, lumberyards, industrial facilities, giant cranes and equipment storage, but there is one place where explorers can take in the vast array of activity. Located at 1 Sitcum Way, near the port's administration building, is a three-story observation tower, open year-round. The tower experience includes interpretive panels that outline the port's history and types of operations it has seen over the years. Guests may want to bring binoculars to see distant cranes loading and unloading ships, but the tower also offers a mounted public pair that anyone can use.

Foss Waterway Seaport

Maritime explorers arriving in Tacoma today can still see some of the original warehouses, docks and waterfront businesses that once secured the city's economic future. In fact, the Foss Waterway Seaport is housed in one of those historic dockside warehouses, and it offers a multi-use experience for visitors. The waterway is named after Tacoma's entrepreneurial maritime matron Thea Foss, who sold a five-dollar rowboat for fifteen dollars in 1889, bought a few more boats with the proceeds and began renting boats for fifty cents a day. Her husband, a carpenter, soon turned his attention to building new boats, and together they launched a maritime empire that evolved into today's Foss Maritime Company.

The seaport, located at 705 Dock Street, is as much a working boat shop as it is a maritime heritage museum housing the greatest collection of marine history in the South Sound. Offering moorage to visiting ships, repairs and refurbishments of vessels and educational opportunities for visitors, Foss Waterway Seaport is a must-see destination for explorers when in Tacoma. Guests can learn more about Thea Foss and the hundreds of tugboats once owned and operated by her company, as well as the area's maritime culture and marine ecology, through art, exhibits and hands-on experiences for all ages.

The five-mile drive from Foss Waterway Seaport out to Point Defiance along the Schuster Parkway and Ruston Way waterfront is teeming with maritime history. Aside from the dozens of seafood restaurants, travelers will find the stretch lined with publicly accessible beaches and parks, nautical sculptures, interpretive panels and more. Mixed among the maritime attractions are working areas with varying purposes. The Department of Agriculture maintains a grain inspection terminal. The two enormous gray vessels that look like battleships docked along the shoreline are the SS *Cape Island* and SS *Cape Intrepid*, owned by the U.S. Department of Transportation's Maritime Administration and on constant standby to deliver emergency supplies to strategic points around the area in the event of a natural disaster, war or other calamity. Ghost pilings from long-gone waterfront businesses poke through the surface at Dickman Mill and Cummings Park, and the historic Point Ruston ferry—a 1936 naval vessel turned Maine passenger transport—is available for tours and rentals. At the end of Point Ruston is the Tacoma Yacht Club, a public boat launch and the ferry terminal that serves the southern end of nearby Vashon Island.

Tacoma's *Fireboat No. 1* served from 1929 to 1982 and was designated a National Historic Landmark in 1989. It is currently on display at Marine Park off Ruston Way. *Tacoma Public Library, Richards Studio D14468-22.*

One of the more interesting historical maritime attractions along the waterfront is the restored *Fireboat No. 1* on permanent display outside Duke's Seafood at 3327 Ruston Way. Built in 1929 to help protect the fledgling Port of Tacoma's wooden wharves and warehouses, it was named a National Historic Landmark in 1980—one of only five fireboats with such a designation. For over fifty years, Tacoma's *Fireboat No. 1* patrolled the waters of Commencement Bay with seven water cannons, providing fire protection and harbor security, conducting search and rescue missions and more.

Visitors to Tacoma's waterfront today can walk completely around the ninety-six-foot hull and marvel at the bright red paint indicative of its firefighting mission. Though maritime enthusiasts can't board the vessel for a closer look, explorers are encouraged to take photos, read the interpretive signs and ponder the significance of it being the only fireboat in U.S. history to singlehandedly protect a major port for more than half a century.

The Puyallup Tribe

Prior to the arrival of the first non-Indigenous people, the area was populated by the Puyallup Tribe (pronounced "pyoo-ALL-up" and anglicized from spuyaləpabš). Known as the "people from the bend at the bottom of the river" for the location of their villages on the banks of what is today the Puyallup River, the tribe spoke Twulshootseed (anglicized from txʷəlšucid), a dialect of Lushootseed spoken by many Indigenous peoples in the Northwest. Their traditional lands extended from the foothills of Mount Rainier (known to them as təqʷuʔma and anglicized as Tahoma) to the shores and islands of Puget Sound. The Puyallup River empties into Commencement Bay, named by Charles Wilkes in 1841 because he began his survey of the area from that bay.

In the mid-1850s, the Puyallup Tribe signed the Medicine Creek Treaty but soon grew dissatisfied with the result, feeling they had been either misunderstood, cheated or flat-out ignored. This led directly to the Treaty Wars that pitted Indians against the U.S. Army and companies of local volunteers. Open hostilities finally ended with a renegotiation of the treaty at Fox Island, which granted local tribes new or expanded reservations and guaranteed them the right to fish in their usual and accustomed places.

That right was not upheld, and Puyallup members had to band together with neighboring tribes to fight for fishing rights in the mid-twentieth century, culminating with the 1974 Boldt Decision enforcing the U.S. government's promises. Since that time, the Puyallup Tribe has been a steadfast steward of its marine resources, engaging in sustainable salmon fishing, shellfish harvesting and habitat protection. They've also branched out into other commercial ventures, such as the hugely successful Emerald Queen Casino located on the Puyallup Reservation between Tacoma and Fife, Washington.

Those interested in learning more about the Puyallup Tribe of Indians and its deep connection to the land and waters of what is now Washington can visit the Puyallup Tribe Culture Center at 3509 East Seventy-Second Street in Tacoma.

Gig Harbor

Easily one of the more picturesque seaside communities in Washington, Gig Harbor received its name in 1841 after Charles Wilkes was unable to bring his ships into the shallow harbor during a particularly fierce storm. Instead, he sought refuge there by taking a gig (a small rowboat attached to a larger ship) from the eighty-eight-foot brig USS *Porpoise*. When he published his map of the region, he included the name Gig Harbor. Of course, the area known as Tua'wILkel (anglicized Twa-wal-kut or Twah-well-kawh) had been used for centuries by the S'Homamish Indians as a village site. Closely related to the Puyallup and Nisqually Tribes, the S'Homamish people—listed as the Gig Harbor Band in an 1879 census—lived independently in cedar plank houses or communally in longhouses that sheltered several families and played host to larger gatherings.

The S'Homamish Indians caught fish returning to spawn in surrounding rivers, dug clams, hunted and were highly regarded as basket weavers—and like all the other seafaring tribes in the Puget Sound region, they employed a well-known method for building canoes. By hollowing out cedar logs that had been burned over a fire, then filling the logs with warm water and hot stones to soften the wood, they could drive crossbars into the cavity to spread it further apart to hold more people and supplies. After the S'Homamish signed the Medicine Creek Treaty along with their Puyallup and Nisqually brethren, the band left the Gig Harbor area and was thought to have been absorbed into neighboring reservations.

Gig Harbor today is a mostly affluent maritime community with several large marinas and two salmon-bearing creeks that empty into the shallow harbor. At low tide, it's easy to see why Wilkes and his crew couldn't navigate their brig into the area, as much of the water drains and exposes the tideflats. That doesn't stop boat owners, however, who keep their numerous sail- and powerboats floating in the water despite the rise and fall. Downtown Gig Harbor is an active destination for maritime explorers, offering shopping, dining and recreation all along the waterfront.

Skansie Shipbuilding and Historic Net Sheds

Known as the Maritime City and incorporated in 1946, Gig Harbor was first settled by Croatian and Scandinavian immigrants looking to practice their trades in the new country. Commercial fishing, boatbuilding and logging dominated the local economy, and the settlers' success drew more of their countrymen to the area. Just after 1900, an immigrant named Peter Skansie, who came from an island off the coast of Dalmatia in present-day Croatia, saw what a gasoline-powered motor could do for a boat and immediately went into business with his brothers. They began by affixing engines to hand- or wind-powered vessels but soon were building vessels from scratch.

Within a brief time, the brothers' boatyard grew to produce ferryboats and fishing vessels called purse seiners, named for a fishing technique used in Croatia that used long nets that could be deployed from the rear of the ship as it motored in a wide circle. With weights holding it down and floats at the top, the net could then be cinched together at the bottom like a drawstring purse and hauled back aboard, capturing massive schools of fish within. In its first year, the company built more than a dozen such ships, and by 1930, the Skansie Shipbuilding Company had developed into a prolific business, turning out more than one hundred seiners, ferries, cannery tenders and yachts.

To house these great fishing nets in the off-season and during repairs, the Skansies and other fishing families constructed several net sheds on the Gig Harbor waterfront. These long, narrow buildings extended far out over the water to allow purse seiners to unravel and detach their nets while moored.

There are more than a dozen historic net sheds lining the waterfront in Gig Harbor, Washington, where fishing vessels were moored, fishing nets mended and equipment stored. *Sreasons7.*

Many of these historic net sheds still line the shores of Gig Harbor, adding to the character of the Maritime City. For several generations, the Skansies continued making ships in Gig Harbor, until 1959, when the company was finally sold to a series of successive owners and eventually became a maintenance facility for one of today's marinas.

One of the last remaining purse seiners manufactured by Skansie Shipyards is the sixty-four-foot *Shenandoah*, launched in 1925. After a lengthy career fishing the waters of the Pacific Ocean, it began falling into disrepair and was donated to the Harbor History Museum in 2000 after the owner's retirement. Since that time, a small army of volunteers, shipwrights, painters, carpenters, engineers and community members has been working hard to restore the near-century-old vessel. With both private and public funding, the work is nearly complete, and the Harbor History Museum expects to unveil the completely restored *Shenandoah* in time for its one hundredth birthday in 2025. Visitors will be treated to an immersive interpretive experience that allows guests to view the ship from all angles, learning about all facets of life above and below the water.

Commercial fishing is no longer the economic driver it once was for Gig Harbor, but it still has great cultural significance to the community. Fortunately for maritime explorers, the Harbor History Museum has installed many historical signs along the Gig Harbor Waterfront History Walk, an interpretive path that takes travelers past several historic net sheds. Within the museum itself, guests can see unique artifacts, historical photos, entertaining and educational videos and interactive exhibits that bring to life the history of the area. On-site are numerous maritime exhibits featuring ferries, tugboats and fishing vessels that once made their home port in Gig Harbor, as well as exhibits featuring Indigenous stories and artifacts from the pre-settlement era. Thanks to support from the City of Gig Harbor, admission to the Harbor History Museum at 4121 Harborview Drive is free.

The Steilacoom Tribe and the Steilacoom Museum

Located about halfway between Tacoma and Olympia is the town of Steilacoom. Pronounced "STILL-uh-cum," this clean and vibrant seaside community takes its name from the Indians who have called this area of Washington home for countless generations. The Steilacoom Tribe is one of only a handful across the state that are not recognized by the federal government, despite a decades-long effort to obtain that designation. This means they have no reservation land, no federal or state support and no special rights guaranteed by the treaties that affected them.

The traditional tribal lands of the Steilacoom people lay in the Tacoma basin area, which stretches from Snake Lake southwest of Tacoma to Sequalitchew Creek just north of DuPont. In addition to just over ten miles of Puget Sound shoreline, it included Anderson, McNeil and Ketron Islands. The Steilacoom Tribe lived among five separate villages—Steilacoom (where the present town is today), Sastuck, Spanaway, Tlithlow and Segwallitchew. These were year-round villages that contained at least one permanent longhouse where villagers would gather. Their families often intermarried but also encouraged relationships with non-Indians, believing that diversity was the key to their survival.

Like many of Washington's Indigenous peoples, the Steilacoom name is an anglicization of a Lushootseed word: in this case, čʼtilqwəbš, the name of a delicate pink flower that grows abundantly in the area. Like all tribal cultures along Washington's coastline, the Steilacoom depended on canoe travel for their food, transportation, relationship building and more. In fact, their origin story tells of a flood so great that it wiped out all the living things on the land, save for one man who managed to get into a canoe and lash it to the top of the highest peak until the floodwaters subsided.

When Isaac Stevens brought the Medicine Creek Treaty to a gathering of more than six hundred Indigenous people on that cold and drizzly gray December morning in 1854, the Steilacoom was one of the dozen or so tribes represented at the gathering. But while their Puyallup, Nisqually and Squaxin Island counterparts were given reservations on which to relocate (albeit of a substandard and unacceptable quality), the Steilacoom Tribe was left out of the agreement because the treaty's framers expected the non-Indian settlement that had developed on Steilacoom land would soon grow into a major shipping port. While the town of Steilacoom can claim the region's first trading post, first church and first U.S. Army fort and was the first incorporated town north of the Columbia River—the "major shipping port" instead materialized to the north, in Tacoma.

The resurgence of canoe culture in the late twentieth century was significant for the Steilacoom Tribe because it helped their people put aside modern burdens and conveniences to reconnect with their heritage in a very personal way. The first Canoe Journey in which the Steilacoom participated, in the mid-1990s, was called the Full Circle Journey. It brought together

The Steilacoom Tribal Cultural Center and Museum operates in a former church building on Lafayette Street in Steilacoom, Washington. *Joe Mabel.*

tribes from deep within Puget Sound and saw them travel north through Admiralty Inlet, west across the Strait of Juan de Fuca and around the tip of Cape Flattery before turning south to traditional tribal lands along the Pacific coast. Since then, the Steilacoom people have been participating in Canoe Journeys almost annually.

Visitors to Steilacoom today can learn more about the Full Circle Canoe Journey and many others at the Steilacoom Tribal Cultural Center and Museum, located at 1515 Lafayette Street in Steilacoom. Operating out of a church building constructed in 1903 and purchased by the tribe in 1987, the cultural center and museum offers guests an intimate look into the history of the Steilacoom people as well as numerous other tribes in the Pacific Northwest. Its gift shop entices visitors to purchase handmade, one-of-a-kind Native art and jewelry, and no photographs are allowed on the second floor out of respect for the photos, stories and artifacts there that help tell the Steilacoom story.

Just blocks away from the tribe's cultural center is the Steilacoom Historical Museum at 1801 Rainier Street, which serves the community by preserving local culture and educating future generations about the heritage of the town of Steilacoom. There are dozens of maritime stories to be found within the exhibits and artifacts at the museum, including descriptions of the area recorded by George Vancouver's lieutenant Peter Puget in his journals; the life of town founder Lafayette Balch (who arrived in 1851 and created a thriving business sailing to San Francisco with lumber and bringing goods back to sell in town); models of prominent ships of the time (including the sidewheel steamer *Fairy*, the first American steamship on Puget Sound that ran between Olympia and Steilacoom); and Steilacoom's era as a resort destination in the late 1800s.

More than just maritime offerings, the Steilacoom Historical Museum Association also maintains several neighboring buildings, including the original home and orchard of early settlers Nathaniel and Emma Orr and a recreation of their family's wagon shop filled with nineteenth-century pioneer tools and implements. The museum features a quaint gift shop, admission is free and donations are appreciated.

HUB CITY: OLYMPIA

Named in 1850 by early settler Edmund Sylvester after he spotted the distant Mount Olympus on the Olympic Peninsula from the shoreline, Olympia was soon designated the capital when Washington became a U.S. territory in 1853. It was subsequently elevated to state capital in 1889 when Washington became the forty-second state to join the Union. Among the collection of monumental structures designed by famed civic architects Wilder and White, visitors to Olympia will find the impressive domed capitol building made of locally quarried and intricately carved sandstone. In addition to being the seat of Washington's government, Olympia is an international trade seaport boasting the seventh-largest marina in the state and a boatworks capable of hauling out vessels up to eighty feet in length and weighing five tons. The port features three deepwater berths, an enormous open beam warehouse and capacity to manage bulk cargo as easily as it does timber.

Located at the extreme southern point of Puget Sound at the end of Budd Inlet, Olympia has long been a maritime-based community. Its earliest residents, members of the Nisqually and Squaxin Island Tribes, would travel by canoe to trade and harvest shellfish in the area prior to non-Indigenous arrival. Within just a few years of their arrival, however, settlers began establishing a permanent presence on the waterfront that soon grew into a booming mill and shipping town.

OLYMPIA WATERFRONT

One of the places that rapidly developed on Olympia's waterfront is Percival Landing, a stretch of commercial and industrial businesses that soon became a busy Mosquito Fleet terminal. At low tide, however, larger ships couldn't reach the existing docks and had to be unloaded onto smaller vessels further up the inlet, an inconvenience at best and a dangerous waste of time at worst. Captain Sam Percival was the first to build a commercial-scale wharf, said to have extended a mile out over the sea, allowing the bigger (and more lucrative) cargo ships to reach the landing without assistance. Tugboats and barges also shuttled ships and cargo around the bay, loading and unloading at the smaller adjacent wharves.

In 1877, Sam Percival turned the business over to his sixteen-year-old son, John, who soon realized that Olympia needed more waterfront to accommodate the growth in maritime business. John collaborated with Mayor P.H. Carlyon and city leaders in 1910 to dredge over two million cubic yards of sediment from the harbor floor and deposited it behind

A.L. Bancroft & Company's bird's-eye view lithograph of Olympia Harbor in Washington Territory, 1879. *Library of Congress, Geography and Map Division.*

bulkheads to expand the northern shoreline by almost thirty blocks. After that, businesses quickly occupied the new land, and Olympia continued to build on its marine-related economic success. This commercial activity is commemorated during the annual Olympia Harbor Days festival on Labor Day weekend in early September, featuring vintage tugboats on display and traditional races on Budd Inlet. The fill area is now occupied by the Port of Olympia and Port Plaza, a beautiful community space at the north end of the Percival boardwalk. Visitors can climb to the top of a three-story wooden viewing tower for the full perspective of Port of Olympia international shipping and tugboat and longshore worker operations.

Several waterfront restaurants are located along Percival Landing, including Budd Bay Café, which features historical tugboat-focused décor developed in partnership with the nonprofit South Sound Maritime Heritage Association (SSMHA), founder of the Harbor Days festival. From the 1920s to the 1970s, the site was home to Delta V. Smyth Tugs & Barges, whose fleet included the tugboats *Sand Man* and *Parthia*. Other popular downtown waterfront area stops include the Olympia Oyster House restaurant, once an oyster-processing plant; Anthony's Homeport and Hearthfire Grill; nearby McMenamins Spar Café, a traditional favorite of both state legislators and tugboat crews; and two craft and art galleries, Childhood's End and Splash.

TUGBOAT HERITAGE WALK

Parthia and *Sand Man* are both historic vessels that will be displayed permanently as part of a year-round Tugboat Heritage Walk, a South Sound feature of the Maritime Washington National Heritage Area. With fundraising nearly complete, *Parthia* will soon be available for public educational (as well as photo) opportunities. A longtime participant in the Harbor Days festival and tugboat races, *Parthia* previously worked in the Olympia harbor for forty years towing ships at the port for Delta V. Smyth as well as Foss Maritime. *Parthia* unexpectedly sank in Hood Canal in 2017, and the tug was donated by its private owner to the SSMHA for restoration and shoreside public exhibit.

The SSMHA accepted the tug, initially funded the project and called on its many maritime history supporters, private companies and nonprofit organizations to help. Local firm Thomas Architecture Studios stepped forward to donate exhibit pavilion design services, and Forma Construction

The tugboat *Sand Man* shown in 1910 moored in Olympia's harbor across from the popular Mosquito Fleet steamer stop at Percival's Dock. *The Sand Man Foundation.*

provided planning and building services. Subsequently, the Port of Olympia approved a permanent site for the tug exhibit at the entrance to the Olympia Farmers Market, adjacent to the Marine Terminal.

Once the *Parthia* is in place, Olympia's newest maritime heritage feature will open to the public. Adventurers will learn more about the city's salty past while strolling the Tugboat Heritage Walk beginning at the *Sand Man* at the south end. Built between 1908 and 1910, the *Sand Man* worked in the Olympia harbor until 1987, when efforts to restore the vessel began. It's now a floating museum ship next to the Olympia Oyster House at 320 West Fourth Avenue.

As visitors continue north along the boardwalk, they'll pass Percival Landing Park and Harbor House, a maritime-themed rentable space adorned with interpretive panels detailing Olympia's history. Continuing along the waterfront will take visitors past seafood restaurants and the marina and onto Port Plaza, where they can get a glimpse of the city's maritime present and future from the observation tower at Port Plaza and read the interpretive panels about Olympia's time as a Liberty Ship port during World War II. After thoroughly exploring the public dock, accessible beaches and maritime art displays, visitors will be able to continue their walk east through the Farmers Market to conclude at the new *Parthia* exhibit. It's sure to be a maritime memory that enthusiasts won't want to miss.

Billy Frank Junior Nisqually National Wildlife Refuge

Experiencing the maritime heritage of the South Puget Sound area must include visiting the Nisqually River delta, named for the Nisqually Tribe that has made its home in the area for countless generations. The dxʷsq̓ʷaliʔ abš, as they're known in Lushootseed, or "People of the Grass, People of the River," were signatories to the Medicine Creek Treaty, the first of many coerced agreements between Isaac Stevens and Washington's Native peoples. Frustration over being relocated to a reservation significantly inland from the tribe's traditional grounds, coupled with ongoing mistreatment by and misunderstandings with non-Indigenous settlers, led to the inevitable conflicts that erupted into the Treaty Wars of 1855–56.

For decades afterward, the Nisqually people tried to live peacefully, harvesting fish from the area's rivers and shellfish, crabs, oysters and other seafood from Puget Sound. Although the Medicine Creek Treaty was renegotiated at the Fox Island Council in 1856, which expanded the size of the Nisqually Reservation, many of the guarantees made to the tribe were not upheld. As more non-Indigenous settlers flooded into the area, even their expanded reservation began to shrink. In 1917, the U.S. Army ordered some of the Nisqually people from their homes without warning and seized the land for a military installation. Later, Pierce County condemned 3,353 acres of the Nisqually Reservation and expanded Fort Lewis.

These kinds of injustices continued into the mid-twentieth century, with Native fishermen being harassed, beaten and arrested for legally exercising their right to harvest salmon from their traditional grounds. One man waged a grassroots effort to fight back against the state and uphold the tribe's guaranteed treaty rights. Billy Frank Jr. was first arrested in 1945, when he was fourteen, after quarreling with game wardens. It would not

The operating historic steamer *Virginia V*, moored at Seattle's South Lake Union Park, is the last of the storied "Mosquito Fleet" of passenger vessels that once crisscrossed the waters of the Puget Sound. *The Steamer Virginia V Foundation.*

Once billed as the largest and most powerful firefighting vessel in the world, the fireboat *Duwamish* is on exhibit at Seattle's South Lake Union Park. It could pump 22,800 gallons of water per minute and fought countless ship and waterfront fires from 1910 until its retirement in 1984. *Seattle Fireboat Duwamish.*

The tiny tug *Wasp* is flanked by the *Arthur Foss* and Lightship No. 83 *Swiftsure* at Historic Ships Wharf on the north side of the Museum of History and Industry in Seattle, Washington. *Northwest Seaport*.

The first of many subsequent Tribal Canoe Journeys, known as the Paddle to Seattle, took place during the Washington state centennial commemoration in 1989. *Washington State Archives*.

A shipwright works on restoring the purse seiner FV *Shenandoah*, on exhibit at the Harbor History Museum in Gig Harbor, Washington. *Ron Rogers, HHM Collection*.

Washington's state centennial tall ship, the *Lady Washington*, takes passengers on historical experience voyages from various ports on the Washington coast and in Puget Sound and is available for free dockside tours. *Grays Harbor Historical Seaport*.

On nearly every beach in Washington, combers can find the wave-worn remains of bricks once used in canneries, mills and other waterfront industrial sites in the nineteenth and early twentieth centuries. *Brian Morris*.

International cargo carriers unload their containers at the Port of Seattle as the tug *Hunter D* stands ready to assist. *Port of Seattle*.

Hanging on the wall of the Center for Wooden Boats boat shop is a collection of both traditional and modern hand tools used to build wooden masterpieces. *Washington Our Home*.

Fleets of fishing vessels have made Fishermen's Terminal in Seattle, Washington, their home port for more than a century. *Port of Seattle*.

Brackett's Landing, the site of the WSDOT ferry terminal in Edmonds, Washington, is one of the best places in the state to see spectacular sunsets over Puget Sound and the Olympic Mountains. *Public domain*.

Fishing—by one species or another—has taken place in Liberty Bay near Poulsbo, Washington, since before recorded time. *David Ayers, USGS*.

Visitors to Tacoma's Old Town neighborhood can see *Fireboat No. 1* on display throughout the year. It had seven water cannon nozzles and the capacity to deliver ten thousand gallons of water per minute to fight waterfront fires. *Joe Mabel.*

Once a popular stop along Seattle's waterfront for Mosquito Fleet steamers, the Coleman Dock burned in the Great Seattle Fire of 1889. It was rebuilt with an iconic seventy-two-foot clock tower, as seen in this 1912 postcard photo. *Public domain.*

The U.S. Naval Undersea Museum in Keyport, Washington, provides a comprehensive look at the navy's undersea activities, including torpedoes, mines, diving and salvage, submarine technology and undersea vehicles. *Washington Our Home*.

Three iconic vessels of distinct types—the 1913 schooner *Adventuress*, the 1922 steamer *Virginia V* and the 1889 tugboat *Arthur Foss*—exemplify Washington's maritime heritage and were honored as State Centennial Flagships in 1989. *Don Wilson Photography*.

Today's Hotel de Haro at the Roche Harbor Resort contains the simple, historic charm of a time gone by and features nineteen appropriately decorated guest rooms. *Washington Our Home.*

Meriwether Lewis and William Clark and their Corps of Discovery expedition have long inspired American artists like Charles Russell, who in 1904 created this watercolor painting of the explorers' first meeting with Chinook Indians. *Public domain.*

Visitors to the *W.T. Preston* sternwheel snag boat in Anacortes, Washington, can explore the National Historic Landmark on their own or take advantage of the volunteer docents who provide guided tours. *Washington Our Home.*

Ship Harbor, named after the warship USS *Massachusetts*, which was stationed there in the 1850s, was once the site of some of the largest and most well-known salmon canneries in the world. *Washington Our Home.*

This marine navigational beacon is located on the southern tip of Point Roberts at Lighthouse Marine Park, one of the best places in Washington State to view whales from land or simply gaze out across the Strait of Georgia. *Klara Steffkova.*

Washington's maritime culture has been the inspiration for countless artists, as evidenced by this Karla Fowler painting of two Foss Maritime tugs assisting the TOTE Maritime cargo ship *Midnight Sun* into the Port of Tacoma. *Karla Fowler.*

Pacific Northwest marine artist Steve Mayo's painting of the fur-trading ship *Columbia Rediviva*, commanded by Captain Robert Gray, is an illustrative depiction of the cross-cultural encounters that occurred over two centuries ago around the Puget Sound. *Steve Mayo*.

Architect's rendering of the restored historic tugboat *Parthia*, shown at its permanent exhibit location near Olympia's waterfront. It is linked with the tug *Sand Man* as part of the Tugboat Heritage Walk. *Thomas Architecture Studio*.

Authentically restored, the more-than-century-old tugboat *Sand Man* is dedicated to teaching residents and visitors about the working maritime history of Olympia and South Puget Sound. *The Sand Man Foundation.*

Built to house a memorial to the Indigenous village buried by a mudslide around 1750, the Ozette longhouse near the archaeological site is maintained by the Makah Indian Nation. *Washington Our Home.*

Ahle Point, just south of Kalama, Washington, continues its historical role as a sternwheeler landing when the *American West*, operated by American Cruise Lines, takes its guests up the Columbia and Snake Rivers. *Washington Our Home.*

The 1918 lighthouse at Lime Kiln State Park on San Juan Island is one of the most picturesque places from which to search for whales, explore the marine environment and learn about state history. *Washington Our Home.*

The Washington State Ferry system maintains the largest fleet in the United States and safely transports nearly fifty thousand riders each weekday. *Brian Morris.*

Westport, Washington, home of the Westport Maritime Museum, shelters commercial and charter fishing vessels in addition to pleasure craft. *Bill Perry.*

Sound Experience out of Port Townsend has been educating, inspiring and empowering youth and adults through the historic schooner *Adventuress* for decades. *Sound Experience.*

The Puyallup River's journey through Pierce County begins at Mount Rainier and ends beside Blair Waterway at the Port of Tacoma on Commencement Bay. *Port of Tacoma.*

be the last time, as Frank continued to peacefully fish where his ancestors had for so many years before European Americans ever set foot in the area. Rising tensions between the state, local tribes and non-Indigenous fishermen led to what's now known as the Fish Wars of the 1960s and 1970s. Frank accumulated more than fifty arrests during his campaign for justice, and it wasn't until the struggle was taken to the courts in *U.S. v. Washington* that federal judge George Boldt issuing a ruling upholding the treaty rights of the Nisqually and other Native tribes in 1974. The Boldt Decision reaffirmed tribal rights to half of the harvestable salmon returning to western Washington and paved the way for Indian tribes in Washington to comanage natural resources in the state.

Frank's activism and determination gave him a place of high stature within the Nisqually Tribe and among other tribes in Washington. When he died in 2014, he was posthumously awarded the Presidential Medal of Freedom by President Barack Obama, and the estuary where Frank and his fellow tribal members had been harvesting resources for millennia—the same place where his people reluctantly agreed to Stevens's dictated

Nisqually fishermen would ply the waters of south Puget Sound in canoes and build weirs across area rivers to catch returning salmon. *Washington State Archives.*

treaty terms—was renamed the Billy Frank Jr. Nisqually National Wildlife Refuge. Within its boundaries today, maritime explorers can stroll the myriad trails through a wide array of natural habitats and view abundant wildlife or hike the mile-long boardwalk that extends to where the river meets the sea. A visitor center at 100 Brown Farm Road in the refuge educates visitors about the history of the Nisqually River delta and the people who lived on it, as well as the natural wonders it contains.

DuPont's Cement Shipwreck

Fifteen miles northeast of Olympia on Interstate 5 is the city of DuPont, originally a company town named for the DuPont Powder Works company, which manufactured explosives there between 1909 and 1975. Its significance in maritime history goes back much farther, however, as it was also the site of the first Independence Day celebration west of the Mississippi River when Charles Wilkes and the crews of the USS *Vincennes* and the USS *Porpoise* commemorated the occasion in 1841. The expedition chose the site for its central location along Puget Sound and later erected a scientific observatory in a small clearing atop the nearby hills. Though the building is long gone, the DuPont company erected a monument on the site in the early twentieth century. It can be reached by hiking the Wilkes Observatory Trail that runs along the bluff.

Another hike that will pique the interest of maritime explorers must be undertaken at low tide, as it leads to a unique shipwreck just off DuPont's coast. Known locally as the Concrete Ship or the Cement Ship, the hundred-foot hulk all but disappears when the tide is in but lies split in two and half-buried in the tideflats when the water is at its lowest. Originally built as a water tender in 1919 by the Great Northern Shipbuilding Company out of Vancouver, Washington, ship number 223169 was given the name *Captain Barker*. Along with its four sister ships, this "stone boat" was to be towed to Fort Stevens, Oregon, and San Francisco, California, by the U.S. Army tug *Slocum*—until three of the ships were lost en route during a nasty storm.

Only the *Captain Barker* and the *Captain Bootes* survived the journey, and both were later sold to the Foss Launch and Tug Company in the 1950s and renamed *Foss 103* and *Foss 102*, respectively. Records don't reveal what happened to the *Captain Bootes*, but the *Captain Barker* appears to have

When the tide is out, beachcombers can explore the wreckage of the 1919 concrete ship *Captain Barker* by taking the Sequalitchew Creek Trail in DuPont, Washington. *Olivia Harrell.*

been lost sometime in the 1970s, sinking to the ocean floor in the very spot it remains today.

This type of ship, known as a ferrocement ship, is constructed with reinforced steel bars encased in concrete, due to the lower cost of these materials compared to more traditional methods. Ferrocement ships were used heavily between World War I and World War II and helped support both United States and British invasions in Europe and the Pacific. Maritime explorers can park at the DuPont Civic Center, 1700 Civic Drive, and hike the nearly two-mile Sequalitchew Creek Trail to the beach. Turning left and hiking along the waterfront for another thirty minutes or so should bring the wreck into view. At a minus tide, the straight path from the beach to the boat is clearly visible, and the wreck is completely exposed and waiting for exploration. Adventurers should be warned, however, not to spend too much time pondering the past, lest the tide come in and trap them aboard the derelict vessel for another twelve hours or so.

Explorers not looking to hike but still interested in local history can visit the DuPont Historical Museum at 207 Barksdale Avenue. Admission is free, and donations are welcome.

HUB CITY: SHELTON

Just over twenty miles northwest of Olympia is the city of Shelton, an industrial community with a hardworking history. Situated at the corner of Oakland Bay and Hammersley Inlet, Shelton is a lumber town, through and through, but has seen both shipping and fishing interests in its time. Founded in 1853 by early settler David Shelton and his family, the town grew in prominence when what would become Mason County was carved out of Thurston County the following year, and Shelton was designated the county seat in 1888. David Shelton's property was in a prime location and soon became the site of a successful lumber mill, railroad line and, later, a wharf that greeted the Mosquito Fleet steamships that brought transportation to town.

In the early 1900s, the Simpson Lumber Company bought out Shelton's timber interests to form the second-biggest timberland owner in the state, behind Weyerhaeuser. For the next half century, the mills in Shelton attracted workers from all over North America, and the community of Shelton developed a reputation as being a raucous place where men worked hard and played harder. The industrial development and willing workforce attracted more companies to Shelton, like Rainier Pulp and Paper, which became Rayonier Incorporated in 1937. Rayonier developed a method to use pulp in new and exciting ways, but it had a terrible side effect in that it generated harmful waste. In addition to its timber operations, Shelton had other agricultural prospects it was developing. One of them was growing oysters commercially, and the waste byproduct from nearby lumber production turned out to be devastating to the oyster beds in Oakland Bay.

The Simpson Lumber Company (which became Simpson Timber Company in 1956) relied on the wharf connected to its mill, as seen here in 1945. Its waterfront location in Shelton, Washington, was critical to its operation for nearly a century before it shut down in 2015. *Public domain.*

Native Americans had been harvesting a species known now as Olympia oysters for centuries prior to non-Indigenous arrival, and when the shellfish became a popular delicacy in big-city eateries, local settlers began to harvest them as well. After 1889, the state allowed anyone to file a claim on tidelands, and both settlers and Indians began "farming" oysters in the bay. Soon, however, they were joined by oystermen from other parts of the state who had overharvested their own beds. The balance of sustainability began to shift, exacerbated by the ongoing industrial pollution, and the result was a sharp decline in Olympia oysters. It wasn't until recently that strategic partnerships developed to help return the oyster beds to a farmable condition. The success of these efforts has significantly boosted the number of harvestable oysters, and the future looks bright for a continued increase in succulent marine mollusks.

Explorers looking for more stories from Shelton's past can visit the Mason County Historical Museum at 427 West Railroad Avenue.

THE SKOKOMISH TRIBE

Just over eleven miles north of Shelton is the Skokomish (pronounced "skoh-KOH-mish") Indian Reservation, home of what is now the Skokomish Tribe of Indians, or the "People of the River." Prior to being relocated to the reservation in the mid-1850s, however, they were known as the Twana Indians, a Salishan people who lived in nine communities within the Hood Canal drainage basin. Before first contact with non-Indigenous people, the tribe subsisted on hunting, fishing and shellfish-gathering activities, moved from place to place with the changing seasons and used the inland waterways for canoe transportation. The biggest of the villages was called Skokomish (anglicized from sqʷuqʷóbəš), which is why both the reservation and the people who live on it are now called that as well.

In the early 1900s, American industrialists bought up land where the Skokomish had traditionally lived for centuries and began changing its face to suit business needs. Diking and ploughing around the Skokomish River caused native plant life to die off, interfered with migrating salmon

Today's Skokomish Tribe is made up primarily of the descendants of the Twana Indians, a nomadic people who subsisted on hunting, fishing and gathering in the Hood Canal basin. *Edward Curtis/Library of Congress.*

and wreaked havoc on the tribe's oyster-farming activities. Two upriver dams built in 1926 and 1930 further worsened the situation by destroying the tribe's important cultural sites. In the 1960s, the tribe sued to protect what land and waterfront they had left—winning a critical victory and financial settlement that they used to improve tribal housing and build a fish-processing plant. When the Boldt Decision affirmed tribal treaty rights in the 1970s, the Skokomish resumed their traditional activities with vigor.

The tribe today has been working to develop collaborative partnerships with area fishing and logging companies, as well as investing in its own future in these industries. In addition to their casino, the Skokomish operate a fish hatchery and began seeding their tideflats again with young oysters in 2018. Their work, along with the work of others who recognize the need for sustainability and balance in nature—like Shelton-based Taylor Shellfish Farms, a family-run business since 1891—has begun to turn the tide on the supply of Olympia oysters in the waters of South Puget Sound.

Maritime explorers who visit the Skokomish Reservation with a full tank of gas and an extra hour and a half can drive the beautiful Highway 101 along the north side of Hood Canal. The drive follows the coastline, passing through wonderfully quaint waterfront communities like Potlatch, named for the Chinook Jargon word meaning "gift giving"; Hoodsport, home of the Hoodsport Winery; Lilliwaup, where a historic shellfish cannery still reaches out over the water; Hamma Hamma, where the fresh, cold waters of the Olympics feed the beds of a century-old oyster company; and Quilcene, the self-proclaimed "Pearl of the Peninsula."

Squaxin Island Tribal Museum, Library and Research Center

Kamilche (pronounced "kuh-MILL-chee") is a small town seven miles south of Shelton and home to the Squaxin Island Tribe, anglicized from sqʷaxsədəbš, meaning "People of the Water." The tribe consists of descendants of several Lushootseed-speaking peoples (the Noo-Seh-Chatl, Steh-Chass, Squi-Aitl, T'Peeksin, Sa-Heh-Wa-Mish, Squawksin and S'Hotle-Ma-Mish). A rich maritime culture, the Squaxin Island Tribe lived and prospered along the shores of the Salish Sea for generations before they were moved onto their four-and-a-half-mile-long island reservation after signing the Medicine Creek Treaty in 1854.

Members of the Squaxin Island Tribe, known as the "People of the Water," continue to be stewards of their marine resources as they work to restore native Salish canoe culture. *Michael Schramm/USFWS.*

As the years passed and the Treaty Wars ended, the small, forested island proved to be a poor home for the 375 Squaxin Island Tribe members, and most families left the island and returned to living near their original homes on Puget Sound. By 1862, the island's population was less than fifty, and today, it is uninhabited. However, the island is still the Squaxin Island Tribe's reservation and is used for sustenance gathering and other activities. It is restricted land, accessible to tribal members and their guests only. Over time, the tribe purchased hundreds of acres on the mainland in Kamilche, where the tribe's headquarters and community is located.

Members of the Squaxin Island Tribe are deeply connected to the water and its resources and are renowned for their skill at canoe carving. When the annual Canoe Journey came to their territory in 2012, the Squaxin Island Tribe welcomed over one hundred canoes to Budd Inlet in Olympia. Today, the tribe has built cooperative relationships with the state to manage the area's marine resources, such as salmon, shellfish, crab and more. Tribal members continue to fish in their usual and accustomed places, as is their right by treaty with the United States, but while following tribal policies, regulations and restrictions.

To help preserve its heritage and celebrate its culture, the Squaxin Island Tribe constructed a museum, library and research center in the early twenty-first century. It is built to resemble Thunderbird, a mythical creature of great power that is central to numerous Native peoples across the continent. Visitors will find themselves immediately immersed in the tribe's maritime culture on entering the museum—known as the Home of Sacred Belongings—which is filled with artifacts, exhibits, photographs, items recovered from archaeological digs and narratives of Squaxin elders. Maritime explorers won't want to miss this enthralling Indigenous experience, located at 150 SE Kwuh-Deegs-Altxw in Kamilche. The tribe requests visitors call before arriving to ensure the museum is ready to welcome them.

PART IV

OLYMPIC
PENINSULA

Jefferson, Clallam and
Grays Harbor Counties

HUB CITY: PORT TOWNSEND

Washington's vast Olympic Peninsula is one of the most naturally beautiful areas in the state and contains some of its remotest locations. Travelers reaching the region by ferry from Whidbey Island are brought to Port Townsend, a community that values its history as much as its creative spirit. The bay on which it sits was originally named Port Townshend by George Vancouver in 1792, after his friend the British Marquis Townshend. The original occupants of the land, members of the Klallam Tribe and other Indigenous bands, called the place Kah Tai and moved in and out of the area with the changing seasons.

After the arrival of the first non-Indian residents between 1848 and 1851, Port Townsend—noted for its well-protected harbor—quickly developed into a bustling port city. Within a few years, it became the official U.S. Customs point of entry for the Puget Sound region, where all foreign ships had to stop before heading to destinations farther south. For fifty-seven years (minus a four-year kerfuffle that temporarily moved the customshouse to nearby Port Angeles), Port Townsend, affectionately called Key City or the New York of the West, was one of the first places immigrants to the United States would set foot on American soil.

In 1893, the federal government finally completed construction on the grand customshouse, court and post office building still standing today at 1322 Washington Street. But its opening coincided with the beginning of a bleak period in the town's history. The nationwide economic crash that same year saw funding for additional projects dry up like driftwood at low tide. As

Immigrants coming to America through Port Townsend, Washington, would have viewed the dock and the first U.S. Customs House (*at right*) as they stepped off their ship. *North Olympic Library System.*

happened in Anacortes, when the Oregon Improvement Company—which had been investing in burgeoning cities in Washington—went bankrupt, all plans for massive expansion to accommodate future growth evaporated. The city's booming population (over six thousand in 1889) quickly dwindled to a few thousand in just over a year. Word soon came that the Northern Pacific Railroad's plan to extend its line from the south Puget Sound area to Port Townsend had been scrapped, marking what many believed was the death knell of a once-promising waterfront community.

The Key City, however, seemed determined not to go down without a fight. Despite the diminished population, lack of stable employment and transfer of the customs headquarters to Seattle in 1911, Port Townsend continued to endure. Slow though the decades were, the city soon welcomed soldiers stationed at the new Fort Worden in the early 1900s. A national company chose Glen Cove near Port Townsend for the site of its new paper mill, bringing both jobs and infrastructure improvements to the city. Perhaps best suited to persevere through economic twists and turns, Port Townsend began attracting artists and architects in the 1960s. Many of the town's

Victorian-era homes were still standing, and residents began to realize their historic value. By the 1970s, both the historic waterfront and the Victorian neighborhood had been added to the National Register of Historic Places and soon after named a National Historic Landmark District, as well.

Port Townsend today features museums, galleries, shops and restaurants and plays host to dozens of festivals, fairs, conferences, conventions and community events, attracting visitors from across the Pacific Northwest and Canada. Despite its growing pains, the Key City seems to have matured to possess the soul of an artist, the heart of a historian and the mind of a tourism marketer, all inside a body of Washington's serene coastal surroundings.

Adventuress and the Northwest Maritime Center

Located at the west end of downtown Port Townsend is the Point Hudson Marina, a forty-five-slip protected waterway with three restaurants and 800 feet of dock for larger vessels. One of the more notable larger ships at Port Hudson is the *Adventuress*, a 133-foot gaff-rigged schooner built in 1913 with the sole purpose of helping its owner hunt a bowhead whale in Alaska. While that mission failed, the *Adventuress* has since lived a long and useful life of service.

After losing interest in whale hunting, *Adventuress*'s owner sold the ship to the San Francisco Bar Pilots Association, where it spent the next three and a half decades shepherding cargo ship pilots across the treacherous shoals of the Farallon Islands, known to mariners as the Devil's Teeth. For a brief time during World War II, *Adventuress* was conscripted into the Coast Guard to help ferry pilots and crews across the San Francisco bar. After being relieved of duty, the two-masted schooner changed hands a few more times, finally relocating to the Pacific Northwest to be used as a sail training vessel for young sailors.

Today, *Adventuress* is owned and operated by the nonprofit group Sound Experience (based out of Port Townsend), which uses the historic ship to educate guests about the beautiful, unique and fragile ecosystem of the Salish Sea. A shining example of living maritime history, *Adventuress* hosts thousands of young sailors each year, helping instill in them a love of the environment and seafaring heritage and teaching them how to be responsible stewards of nature's gifts.

One of three state centennial flagships designated in honor of Washington state's one hundredth birthday, the 1913 schooner *Adventuress* now serves as a floating classroom to teach environmental stewardship on Puget Sound. *Elizabeth Becker/Sound Experience.*

The best place to learn more about ships like *Adventuress* and others is Port Townsend's Northwest Maritime Center, 431 Water Street. The center's campus-like facility provides visitors with a multitude of ways to experience contemporary maritime life. Billing itself as a "big tent" organization that encompasses everything related to boats and the sea, the Northwest Maritime Center is the place to be for marine enthusiasts. It offers dozens of types of sail training and camps for youth and adults, Coast Guard credentialing classes, vocational training for future professional mariners, a voluminous research library and a boat shop that grants space to community woodworkers and boatbuilders. The center sponsors several annual boat races and regattas and hosts events and festivals throughout the year, like the Port Townsend Wooden Boat Festival—a Northwest favorite since 1977. Of course, there's also a small museum and gift shop where explorers can buy a reminder to bring home of their remarkable experience under the big tent of the Northwest Maritime Center.

Fort Worden and Point Wilson Lighthouse

Bordering Port Townsend's northern end is Fort Worden, the second point in Washington's Triangle of Fire (along with Forts Casey and Flagler). Like its siblings, Fort Worden served a vital coastal defense purpose until reaching the age of obsolescence, after which the federal government transferred ownership of the property to the Washington State Parks system.

Within the boundaries of Fort Worden are several museums maritime enthusiasts will want to visit. The nonprofit group Friends of Fort Worden has taken great care to create a wonderful experience for visitors of any age. From the fort's office and gift shop at 200 Battery Way, travelers can pick up a self-guided walking tour map that will lead explorers to the Commanding Officer's Quarters Museum. One of the fort's most lovingly restored buildings, the museum is a fine recreation of how an officer's family would have lived, complete with late Victorian and Edwardian furniture. The 1904 building closest to the waterfront along Officer's Row on Pershing Avenue was home to many different families over the years, and admission is by donation.

Another gem within Fort Worden State Park is the Puget Sound Coast Artillery Museum, set in Building 201, an original 1904 barracks, next to the park office. Established in 1976 to preserve and interpret the story of Washington's coastal defense network, the museum also includes exhibits about the fort's postwar history, including its brief service as an adolescent treatment center and transition to a state park. Travelers should call ahead to verify hours and admission prices.

One of the more interesting maritime features of Fort Warden is the 1914 Point Wilson Lighthouse, located at the very end of Harbor Defense Way. George Vancouver named Point Wilson in 1792 after his colleague Captain George Wilson. The history of the 1914 building begins in 1879, when the first iteration of the light station was constructed, but decades of beach erosion threatened the original structure, and its replacement came about thirty-five years later. The structure is now undergoing extensive renovation and repair, courtesy of the nonprofit U.S. Lighthouse Society at Point Wilson, but is open for tours on Saturdays and Sundays from eleven to four o'clock. Donations are graciously welcomed, as restoring a historic lighthouse is a worthwhile—albeit laborious and exceptionally costly—endeavor.

Finally, if military and maritime heritage simply doesn't pique a visitor's interest, Fort Worden is also home to the Port Townsend Marine Science

Center, an educational and scientific organization devoted to inspiring conservation of the Salish Sea since 1982. Located at the end of a long pier along the southeastern coastline of the fort property, the center helps tell the story of the area's habitat and marine history with an aquarium, museum and gift shop. Access to any Washington State Park requires purchase of a Discover Pass, which can be obtained online or on location from a kiosk in the main parking area.

Fort Flagler and the Marrowstone Lighthouse

To get to Fort Flagler, the third military installation in the Triangle of Fire guarding the entrance to Puget Sound, explorers leaving Port Townsend need only head south to Port Hadlock-Irondale and turn east, following Highway 116. Located at the northern tip of Marrowstone Island, Fort Flagler Historical State Park's 1,451 acres are surrounded on three sides by water and offer visitors nearly four miles of beach and over a dozen interpretive trails to enjoy.

Like Forts Casey and Worden, Fort Flagler features numerous concrete gun batteries across the property and enough spooky underground bunkers to chill the blood of even the bravest explorers. It's easy to imagine the fort bustling with military activity over a century ago with so many original structures still intact. The parade grounds are surrounded by historical barracks, officer housing, light stations, powerhouses and even the fort's 1905 hospital, which can be toured on Saturdays and Sundays at eleven thirty for a donation.

Fort Flagler's military museum features displays about the area and its history, including pieces of an intertwined metal submarine net that was once strung across Admiralty Inlet to prevent underwater incursions. There are replicas of various munitions fired from Flagler's gun batteries, scale models of the installation and a recreated signal and strategy room on display at the museum, which also includes a small gift shop. Volunteer docents are on hand to answer any questions. Those looking for a more detailed journey of discovery can pick up a map of the historic gun emplacements and other key sites around the property or enjoy a guided walking tour provided by one of the park's knowledgeable interpretive staff for a small donation.

The guns on display at Battery Thomas Wansboro at Fort Flagler State Park are not original to the installation but were relocated from Fort Wint in 1963 to enhance the site's historic atmosphere. *Washington Our Home.*

Once finished exploring the fort's bunkers and batteries, recreationalists will be delighted to know the island is also an ideal place to go camping, fishing, clamming, crabbing, boating, birdwatching, picnicking, wildlife watching, kayaking and even paragliding for thrill-seekers. At the northeastern end of the island is the Marrowstone Point Lighthouse, composed of a six-room keeper's quarters, a bell and signal tower, a woodshed and a boathouse. First constructed in 1896, the facility witnessed the rescue of several unfortunate vessels that ran aground in nearby waters throughout the years, until it was replaced by a new light and fog signal in 1917. Finally automated in 1962, the facility now serves as a guesthouse for visiting U.S. Geological Survey scientists, who use the property as a marine field station. While the fenced areas remain off-limits, visitors are free to explore the beachfront to their heart's content.

THE JAMESTOWN S'KLALLAM TRIBE

One of the most interesting destinations a maritime traveler from Port Townsend should include on their itinerary is the Jamestown S'Klallam property in nearby Blyn just twenty-five miles to the west at the tip of Sequim (pronounced "SKWIM") Bay. Known as the "Strong People" and anglicized from nəxʷsƛ̓áy̓əm, the tribe is closely related to the Port Gamble S'Klallam and the Lower Elwha Klallam. Signers of the 1855 Point No Point Treaty, this band also resisted relocation to the Skokomish reservation some fifty miles to the south.

Instead, the tribe made an unprecedented decision to adopt a new value system that included property ownership. Under the leadership of a tribal citizen named Lord James Balch, members pooled their resources and purchased a 210-acre plot of land along the Strait of Juan de Fuca in 1874. Calling it Jamestown, these members of the S'Klallam Tribe began building their strong, self-reliant community anew. By the 1930s, the federal government began insisting that the tribe relocate to either the Skokomish

For countless generations, members of the Jamestown S'Klallam Tribe have fished the waters of Sequim Bay and the Salish Sea, as they continue to do today. *Chris Burns/ Jamestown S'Klallam Tribe Digital Archives and Museum.*

or Port Gamble reservations and threatened the Jamestown S'Klallam with non-recognition—a threat it ultimately carried out in the 1950s. This led to a legal unification of the three S'Klallam bands, who sued to regain the rights promised them in the Point No Point Treaty. Their arduous work and perseverance paid off in 1981, when the federal government finally relented, granting them full recognition and a restoration of benefits.

The Jamestown S'Klallam Tribe has maintained an unbroken history of seafood harvesting and sale throughout its journey. Tribal fishermen and women today continue to reap nature's benefits by harvesting oysters, clams, crab and geoduck (pronounced "GOOEY-duck" from the Lushootseed word gʷídəq)—the largest and longest-living species of burrowing clam and a delicacy for seafood lovers. Business enterprises such as Jamestown Seafood and Point Whitney Shellfish reflect a heritage that goes back thousands of years and will continue to help drive the community toward a sustainable future.

Today's Jamestown S'Klallam homeland is one of the most scenic and artistically beautiful in the state. Buildings decorated with colorful traditional artwork and Native carvings are abundant throughout the area, and the natural scenery surrounding them is second to none. Visitors are of course invited to enjoy the Seven Cedars Hotel and Casino in Blyn, but heritage enthusiasts may find the Northwest Native Expressions art gallery and gift shop more appealing. Those interested in deepening their knowledge of the Jamestown S'Klallam Tribe may be interested in visiting the tribal library or the House of Seven Generations online photo and artifact collection—a virtual museum found at www.jamestowntribe.org.

HUB CITY: PORT ANGELES

If Clallam County is the crown atop Washington's Olympic Peninsula, then Port Angeles is the crown jewel. Long populated by the Klallam people, the site of today's city was first occupied by two villages, Tse-whit-zen and I'e'nis, before the entirety of it was claimed for Spain by the explorer Francisco de Eliza in 1791. He named the harbor Puerto de Nuestra Señora de Los Ángeles, or Port of Our Lady of the Angels. It wasn't until the mid-nineteenth century that non-Indigenous settlers began moving to the area and started fishing, whaling and trading, eventually shortening the settlement's name to Port Angeles.

Its fluctuating prosperity over the years has led to varying successes, but its deep harbor and location behind the protected shores of Ediz Hook—a natural sandspit extending over three miles out into the Strait of Juan de Fuca—makes it an ideal spot for beachcombing, hiking and wildlife-watching opportunities. At the end of the hook is a public boat ramp and the guarded gates of U.S. Coast Guard Air Station Port Angeles, a facility with multiple helicopter landing pads, an aircraft runway and varying sizes of Coast Guard vessels.

Port Angeles is also the site of a privately operated marine shuttle service run by the historical Black Ball Ferry Line to Victoria, British Columbia, in Canada. Various iterations of the Black Ball company have been around since 1818, when a group of Quakers from New York formed the Wright, Thompson, Marshall & Thompson Line using a maritime flag depicting a black circle on a red background. The company name was a mouthful; it soon became known simply as the Old Line and, after the 1840s, the Black Ball Line. The company turned the global shipping industry on its head by putting its ships on a set schedule. Prior to this, ships often sat in port until their holds were full before departing—an extremely inconsistent and unreliable system.

Seventy-six years later, in the 1880s, one of the founders' grandsons moved to Port Townsend, bringing with him the Black Ball maritime flag and establishing the Alaska Steamship Company. Decades later, it merged with the Puget Sound Navigation Company and continued sailing its ferries under a red flag with a black circle. One of those ships, the MV *Kalakala* (built in 1935), was a unique and luxurious vessel featuring a streamlined hull and art deco stylings. *Kalakala* was the first ship of its kind in the world and extremely popular with both locals and tourists. In 1951, world famous singer-actor (and Washington native) Bing Crosby—along with the Andrews Sisters and the Vic Schoen orchestra—commemorated the company with a catchy tune called "Black Ball Ferry Line," recordings of which can be found on YouTube.

Later that same year, a labor dispute resulted in the company selling its entire Washington ferry fleet to the state's Department of Transportation, ending the era of private ferry service on the Sound. Resigning itself to strictly Canadian operations, Black Ball owners commissioned a new ferry in 1959, the MV *Coho*, sold the rest of their assets to the Canadian government in 1961 and have masterfully maintained a daily, year-round vehicle and passenger ferry run between Port Angeles and downtown Victoria ever since.

The Lower Elwha Klallam Tribe's Carnegie Museum

Located in downtown Port Angeles is the Museum at the Carnegie, in a building that was once one of 2,509 libraries built with money donated by Scottish American businessman and philanthropist Andrew Carnegie between 1883 and 1929. It served as the town's primary library from 1919 to 1998. After the city completed renovations in the early 2000s, the building was rededicated for heritage preservation, and a new tenant—the Lower Elwha Klallam, anglicized from ʔéʔɬxʷaʔ nəxʷsx̣̱ʼáyʼəm—moved into the upper floor.

Known as the "Strong People," like their Jamestown and Port Gamble S'Klallam kin, the Lower Elwha Klallam Tribe, original signers of the Point No Point Treaty in 1855, has resided along the shores of what is now the Strait of Juan de Fuca for thousands of years. The tribe took advantage of the opportunity to showcase its history and way of life at the new Carnegie Museum, located at 205 South Lincoln Street, and created an impressive interpretive space to help tell the story of its culture. Note, however, that the museum is open by appointment only, so travelers will need to call or e-mail the tribe in advance of a visit in person.

One of the most striking exhibits at the museum is of the ancient village of Tse-whit-zen (anglicized from čix̌ʷícən and pronounced "ch-WHEET-son"), an archaeological discovery made in 2003. As state Department of Transportation crews excavated a site along the waterfront at the base of Ediz Hook, they began unearthing as many as eight longhouses, ceremonial areas, prehistoric artifacts, the village's cemetery and other evidence of a once-vibrant community site. Construction was soon abandoned as researchers dating the site discovered it to be around 2,700 years old. They

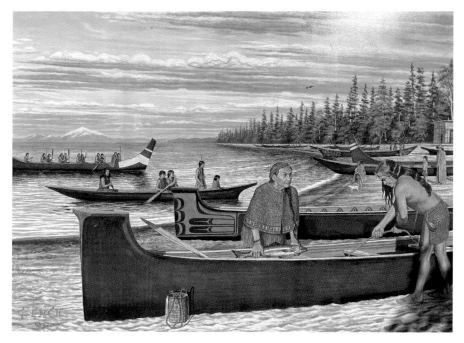

A large mural by internationally known artist Cory Ench near the Port Angeles waterfront depicts a Klallam Native village and its many maritime activities in 1750. *Washington Our Home.*

would soon realize that Tse-whit-zen is the largest pre–European contact village site ever excavated in Washington.

Scientists also learned that the Lower Elwha Klallam Tribe, like most Indigenous peoples in Washington, had been decimated by previously unseen diseases after contact with Europeans. By the time the growing American industrial era reached the 1930s, the tribe's numbers were so few that its surviving members had little choice but to abandon Tse-whit-zen—their ancestral home since the foundation of the Roman Empire. Waterfront lumber mills soon buried the village under more than a dozen feet of fill to make room for more industry, and the village site all but vanished. It is interesting to note, then, that it took another industrial undertaking in the new millennium to uncover what industry had concealed nearly a century earlier.

Over fifty thousand artifacts have been unearthed from the village site, some of which are on display at the Lower Elwha Klallam Museum at the Carnegie. Still others are on display at the nearby Elwha Klallam Heritage Center, which helps needy families, offers vocational training and provides rentable community space. The rest are housed indefinitely at the University of Washington's Burke Museum in Seattle until they can come home again to be with their people.

Feiro Marine Life Center

The city pier in downtown Port Angeles is an excellent place to have a leisurely stroll, take pictures atop the observation tower or enjoy a community festival or market. It's also the location of one of the area's hidden gems— the Feiro Marine Life Center, named after Arthur Feiro, an inspirational teacher and mentor and the driving force behind the center's creation in the 1980s. Located at 315 North Lincoln Street, the center is more than just an aquarium; it's a scientific teaching laboratory that provides the public with a display of marine organisms and ecosystems.

Visitors to the center can get their hands wet in the touch tanks filled with sea stars, hermit crabs, sea cucumbers and more. Guests can learn from volunteer naturalists about the marine life of the north Olympic Peninsula. At the microscope station, kids can learn more about how plankton feeds the world's oceans or talk with a naturalist about the best times and places to explore the area's tide pools. There's even a small gift shop for souvenirs.

SEQUIM MUSEUM AND THE
NEW DUNGENESS LIGHTHOUSE

About halfway between Port Angeles and Port Townsend (as the seagull flies) is the city of Sequim. Pronounced "SKWIM," this hamlet nestled along Highway 101 is famous for its lavender farms and its unique climate. Because it lies within the rain shadow of the Olympic Mountains, it receives an average of less than sixteen inches of rain per year, despite being surrounded by some of the wettest environment in the state. The copious amount of sunshine has led to the nickname Sunny Sequim, and it remains a popular getaway destination for both Washingtonians and Canadians alike.

Just north of the city is Dungeness Spit, the longest natural sandspit in the United States. Like Ediz Hook in Port Angeles, the five-mile-long strip of land extends far into the Strait of Juan de Fuca. It provides shelter for Dungeness Bay and several small communities along the waterfront. Home to the Dungeness National Wildlife Refuge, the spit is contained between the Dungeness Recreation Area on the southern end and the historic New Dungeness Lighthouse at the northern tip. The area was named in 1792 by George Vancouver because it reminded him of Dungeness Point on England's southeast coast—but the experiences at this location are uniquely North American.

First lit in 1857, the New Dungeness Lighthouse consisted of a keeper's dwelling, a boathouse, a fog bell and a few other structures. The lighthouse—and the spit on which it resides—has seen its share of Washington history through the years, as lighthouse custodians have assisted with numerous shipwrecks and stranded vessels and saved the building from fast-moving grass fires on more than one occasion. Long used as a camping ground for Indigenous tribes traveling across the strait, Dungeness Spit was also the site of an 1868 battle between Tsimshian and S'Klallam Indians that resulted in seventeen deaths and one of Washington's most fascinating, if gruesome, historical stories.

Tsimshian Indians were known to raid local tribes, kidnapping women and children and taking them north to become slaves. In early 1868, a S'Klallam man named Lame Jack had one of his wives and a son stolen by Tsimshians and never received compensation for the loss—an expectation among tribes in the Salish Sea. When a band of northern Indians camped at Dungeness Spit on their way home, Lame Jack took advantage of the opportunity to exact his revenge. Collecting twenty-five of his fellow tribesmen, Lame Jack

First in operation in 1857, the "old" New Dungeness Lighthouse survived until 1927, when structural degradation forced the tower to be lowered by thirty-seven feet, to its current height. *Department of Commerce, Bureau of Lighthouses.*

led a midnight raid on the Tsimshian camp, killing the entire party—or so they thought. One pregnant Tsimshian woman survived and made her way undetected to the New Dungeness Lighthouse, where the keeper, Henry Blake, took her in and treated her injuries.

Over fifty years later, in 1920, lighthouse keeper Edward Brooks answered the knock at his door to find a Tsimshian man who had traveled there in a dugout canoe. That man claimed he was the child born to the sole survivor of what became known as the Dungeness Massacre. Brooks told the man that Henry Blake's son, who was present when his father provided refuge to the injured woman, lived across the bay and would be delighted to meet him. The Indian told Brooks that he would visit, but for whatever reason, he instead paddled back to his homeland and never returned.

There is much more to this tale from along Washington's coastline and more information about the New Dungeness Lighthouse, as well. These stories can be found at the Sequim Museum, 544 North Sequim Avenue.

The museum's exhibit *Journey Through Time* details the area's rich maritime history, from its original residents, the Jamestown S'Klallam, to the Wilkes expedition and beyond. It covers the evolution of Washington Harbor, Port Williams, New Dungeness and Old Town and tells the stories of the notable sailing ships and steamers that have worked the waters along Washington's north Olympic coastline through the centuries.

HUB CITY: NEAH BAY

Explorers who enjoy a scenic road trip will want to make the trek out to Neah Bay, near Cape Flattery, the extreme northwestern corner of the contiguous United States. This pristine maritime destination is often overlooked on account of its distance from bigger cities like Port Angeles but is absolutely worth a visit, especially for travelers in search of peaceful solitude or natural wonders. Taking Highway 112 west along the Strait of Juan de Fuca will supply drivers with constantly amazing panoramas of the shoreline while they leisurely wind between enormous rock formations and towering evergreen trees. In contrast to the sunny weather in Sequim's rain shadow, the northern coastline is often smothered by fog or drizzling rain. But on clear days, the views are almost unbeatable as adventurers head toward the end of the highway.

Cape Flattery, the oldest permanently named feature in Washington, was first described in 1778 by British captain James Cook, who noted that its small opening flattered him with hopes of finding a safe harbor (he didn't). Within sight of the cape is Tatoosh Island and the Cape Flattery Lighthouse, a maritime attraction built in 1854 and reachable only by ship or helicopter. Though no longer in service, like most of Washington's iconic light stations, the lighthouse was once flanked by more than a dozen buildings. Several keepers and their families have called Tatoosh Island home, and some are even buried on the island. Over the years, the harsh weather, remote location and a few irresponsible lighthouse tenders caused the structures to degrade to the point that the site was finally automated in 1977, and the island bid farewell to its last full-time residents. In 2008, a solar-powered LED atop a thirty-foot tower replaced the automated beacon, and the remaining structures were turned over to the Makah Tribe, now the caretakers of the island and its small cemetery.

The Makah Indian Tribe and Cultural Center

Though it has had various names since it was first explored by British captains John Mears and Charles Duncan in 1788, the ancestral home of the Kwih-dich-chuh-ahtx (anglicized from qʷidiččaʔa·tx̌ or "People of the Cape") is named after an influential chief named Dee-ah, pronounced "Neah" in their native language. Known today as the Makah, or "People Who Are Generous with Food," the tribe is a federally recognized signatory to the Treaty of Neah Bay, an 1855 agreement with the federal government that required them to relinquish three hundred thousand acres of land in exchange for guaranteed rights to continue hunting whales, seals and fish and other traditional practices. Historically, as with other Indigenous tribes in Washington, those rights weren't usually upheld.

The prospect of hunting whales may seem contrary to modern thinking, but it is a practice that goes back millennia for the Makah people. So important to their culture is whaling that it was explicitly outlined in the Treaty of Neah Bay. Whale hunting provides a purpose for Makah tribal members, and the proceeds benefit the entire community in numerous ways. For generations, whales have provided the Makah with meat, oil, bone, sinew and other resources. The relationship between the Makah and whales is ancient; their tribal logo is a bird carrying a whale in its talons. Yet in the 1920s, commercial whaling had depleted the population of humpback and gray whales. All hunting was subsequently banned.

It wasn't until the late 1990s, when the gray whale was removed from the endangered species list, that the Makah insisted on their treaty-guaranteed whaling rights. In 1999, in a much-publicized event, with the support of the International Whaling Commission and the federal government, the Makah conducted their first traditional whale hunt in over seventy years, successfully hunting and harvesting a gray whale. The endeavor was not without challenges. The Makah method of hunting whale, a tradition passed down orally for generations, involves dozens of men in cedar canoes. Hunters must

The Makah Tribe has a long history of hunting whale for sustenance, as seen in this 1910 Asahel Curtis photo titled *The King of the Seas in the Hands of the Makahs*. *Library of Congress*.

time the breathing of the beast to determine where it will next surface and be prepared to thrust a sixteen-foot flexible harpoon carved from yew into the animal at just the right moment. Trying to avoid the whale's thrashing tail, the hunters must attach inflated seal skins to the whale to slow it down enough to deliver a fatal strike. One tribal member must dive into the water to tie the whale's mouth shut, lest it ingest enough seawater to sink it to the bottom of the ocean. Then, the men in canoes must tow the great carcass to shore, sometimes for miles, before delivering it to the rest of the tribe, who are waiting to process it.

The traditional lands of the Makah stretch across the northwestern tip of Washington and down the coastline, encompassing the five major villages of Osett, Dia'th, Wa'atch, Tsoo-yess and Ba'adah. The best place to learn about these villages, the people and their heritage is at the Makah Cultural Center in Neah Bay, open every day from ten to five o'clock. Visitors to the museum and research center are welcomed by two sentinels watching over the site: carved wooden representations of Makah Indians in traditional clothing, each standing several dozen feet tall. Opened in

1979, the Makah Cultural Center houses and interprets artifacts from the five villages, but none more thoroughly than what is now known as the Ozette archaeological site.

Sometime between the 1500s and 1700s, Makah residents of Ozette were going about their daily lives when a rain-soaked hillside suddenly broke loose and buried the village under feet of mud and debris. Generation after generation passed until the 1970s, when a fierce storm finally began revealing what nature had wiped out centuries earlier. The Makah then partnered with archaeologists from Washington State University to begin painstakingly uncovering the remains of their once-vibrant village. During the yearslong dig, teams discovered several houses with their contents mostly intact and recovered over fifty-five thousand artifacts representing many activities of the Makah, from whale and seal hunting to salmon and halibut fishing to children's toys and games.

Hundreds of these items can be seen in person by travelers willing to trek out to the center at Neah Bay, along with showcases, dioramas, full-size canoes and a longhouse. These artifacts, photographs and exhibits interpret Makah culture and history and feature numerous examples of traditional clothing, basketry and carvings, as well as an ethnobotanical garden containing many specimens of native plant life.

Wedding Rocks and the Ozette Memorial

The truly adventurous should consider backtracking fifteen miles from Neah Bay to Hoko River State Park and turning southwest toward Ozette Lake. From the ranger station on the north shore, it's only a two-and-a-half-mile hike through spectacular coastal forest to the beach at Sand Point, a popular albeit remote pack-in camping destination. Explorers who make it that far can then turn north onto the Pacific Northwest Trail to make their way to an incredibly special, ancient place. Roughly one and a half miles up the coastline are the Wedding Rocks, a series of petroglyphs believed to have been carved by the original residents of Ozette village.

These rocks are so named because of one carving showing what appears to be a man and a woman. Thought by some to represent fertility, the "wedding rock" itself is in two pieces after it split in half during a violent storm in the late twentieth century. There are more than forty petroglyphs at the site, the most striking of which depict faces, orcas and even a sailing

Carved by the Native inhabitants of Ozette Village at Cape Alava, some of the Wedding Rock petroglyphs have been dated to three and five hundred years ago. *Aliaksei Baturytski.*

ship believed to have been a more "recent" addition—carved shortly after the British arrived in 1788. The Ozette Ranger Station is a good place to grab an interpretive guide before trekking out to the beach.

In recent years, however, vandalism of this sacred site has become increasingly destructive. Defacing these centuries-old depictions violates archaeological resource protection laws as well as the cultural heritage of the Makah Tribe. Visitors to the Wedding Rocks site will take note that under the Archaeological Resources Protection Act, vandalism is punishable by up to two years in prison and/or a $20,000 fine, and the site should only be explored with an appropriate reverence.

Continuing up the beach another mile or so toward Tskawahyah Island and Cape Alava, the westernmost point in the contiguous United States, beachcombers will find another site deserving of extreme reverence. Just past the decaying shell of an abandoned waterfront ranger station is another building nestled into the cliffs above the waves. It is a small, weathered longhouse constructed by the Makah Tribe as a memorial to their ancestors who lost their lives in the Ozette mudslide. Where the ranger station looks out of place, hanging precariously over the eroding cliff, the longhouse looks as if it belongs there, having grown up with the grasses and trees that surround it.

Walking from Wedding Rocks to the longhouse, travelers will have crossed from public land to the Makah reservation, and there is no trail or directional signage leading visitors to the building. However, within the structure itself is an oxidized bronze plaque describing how the tragedy at Ozette (spelled Osett) has given rise to a new understanding for the Makah people. Through the archaeological study of the site, the Makah have gained a greater appreciation of the wisdom of their forefathers and a renewal of their desire to strengthen their culture. The walls and floor of the longhouse are adorned with hundreds of bones, from tiny bird skulls to seal ribs to whale vertebrae the size of tree stumps. It is reflective of the gifts that the ocean has provided for the Makah from generation to generation, and anyone visiting the site is advised to take only memories and leave only footprints.

The Quileute and Hoh Tribes

To continue south along Washington's western coastline from Ozette Lake, maritime explorers have two options: either hike the Pacific Northwest Trail or backtrack to the Strait of Juan de Fuca Highway and drive southwest to the community of La Push. This area of the state is home to the Quileute Nation, anglicized from kʷòʔlíyoť, an Indigenous tribe that was once spread across eight hundred thousand acres from the glaciers of Mount Olympus to the rivers of the rain forests. The Quileute story holds that a wandering shapeshifter changed a pack of wolves into their ancestors and that a great flood once swept away the Chimacum band of their tribe across the peninsula to the area near Port Townsend. Being a coastal tribe, the Quileutes had several encounters with non-Indigenous sailors prior to the tribe's signing of the Treaty of Quinault River in 1855 and the Treaty of Olympia the following year.

Quileute tradition holds that their earliest outside contact was with Spanish sailors who shipwrecked somewhere north of La Push, and tribal oral history is rich with European and Asian encounters. A French side-wheel paddle steamer once wrecked near the mouth of the Quillayute River, and the crew lived there for many years, calling the area La Bouche—

meaning "the mouth"—which evolved into the name La Push. In 1787, a small British crew landed near Destruction Island. American explorers traded for furs with the village of La Push in 1792. Even Russian sailors ran aground north of the river in 1808.

Today's Quileute Tribe has created a destination-based economy that offers travelers a peaceful respite on the shores of the Pacific Ocean. The tribe operates an oceanside resort, an RV park, a marina and numerous recreational opportunities, including Rialto Beach, a picturesque collection of sea stacks, driftwood and unique geological formations. In fact, standing sentinel over the river delta is James Island, also known as A-Ka-Lat, or "Top of the Rock." It was the location of a fortified village and is a source of spiritual power for the Quileute people, as well as the burial ground for notable members of the tribe.

Adventurers exploring the reservation may be interested in hiking the Pacific Northwest Trail to investigate a pair of seaside memorials. About three and a half miles north of Rialto Beach is a discreet plaque adorning a concrete block nestled in the undergrowth, a reminder of a tragic shipwreck that left only two survivors. In the winter of 1920, a brutal storm caught the passengers and crew of the Chilean schooner *W.J. Pirrie* by surprise, tossing the ship about until its hull split in two. Eighteen of the twenty souls on board perished in the accident; the surviving two were rescued from the brink of death by Quileute passersby. The monument, only accessible on foot or by sea, notes the exact date of the wreck and lists the names of those who died—all of whom were buried in a mass grave near where the marker lies before being relocated and given proper burials.

Another six and a half miles north along the trail lies a marker commemorating yet another shipwreck in Washington's history. A nighttime storm in January 1903 obscured the navigation of a Norwegian bark, the *Prince Arthur*, en route to British Columbia. The vessel struck a reef and began breaking apart, sending its crew of twenty into the crashing surf. As wave after wave pounded the *Prince Arthur*, sailors searched desperately for anything floating as they made their way toward shore. By the time the sun rose the next morning, only two men had survived the horrific accident. With the help of local Indians, they recovered twelve bodies and buried them in the sandy beach. When word of the tragedy spread to Seattle, that area's tight-knit Norwegian community rallied together and traveled out to the site to transfer the bodies to a more appropriate gravesite on a nearby bluff overlooking the water. In 1904, they etched the names of their fallen countrymen into a granite obelisk and installed it just above the waterline where the bodies had been buried. The site is about ten miles south of Cape Alava and is roughly halfway between the Makah reservation and the Quileute reservation.

From La Push, drivers must backtrack once again to the town of Forks and head south along Highway 101 to reach the mouth of the Hoh River and the Hoh Indian reservation. The Hoh Indians are considered a band of the Quileutes and are also a separate federally recognized tribe. Like their northern river kin, the Hoh have existed for generations by carving canoes for ocean travel; fishing for smelt, salmon and perch; and harvesting clams, crab and other resources from the tidelands. Their reservation contains one of the more dramatic vistas on the Pacific coast at Ruby Beach.

About three and a half miles off the coast of Ruby Beach is Destruction Island, one of many small rocky outcroppings dotting the Olympic coastline left over from prehistoric lava flows and receding Ice Age glaciers. This thirty-three-acre island rises roughly eighty feet above the surrounding water and is bordered by steep bluffs on all sides. Though named due to the ill fortune experienced by early Spanish and British

Pacific coast tribes have long been the stewards of places like Ruby Beach in what is now the Olympic Coast National Marine Sanctuary. *Nick Zachar, NOAA.*

explorers while anchored nearby, the island today is known as the home of the decommissioned Destruction Island Lighthouse.

The lighthouse's ninety-two-foot brick tower was covered with a protective cast-iron casing and housed a first-order Fresnel lens in the lantern room when it first went into operation in 1892. Given its critical role in helping vessels in distress, there were usually four keepers assigned to the station with their families. That necessitated several support buildings, including several keepers' quarters, a fog signal building and water and fuel storage buildings. By 1900, the small community had its own school, grew vegetables and raised cattle to supplement the rations delivered to the island.

The Coast Guard took ownership of the lighthouse in 1939 and began maneuvering to close it by the 1960s. It was finally automated in 1968, but the first-order lens continued rotating endlessly until it was replaced by a modern maritime navigational beacon and relocated to Westport in 1995. That lens is housed at the Westport Maritime Museum in a building showcasing the 130-year-old lens's dazzling display from all angles. The lighthouse tower from which it was taken, however, will only remain standing guard over Destruction Island until time and the elements put it mercifully to rest.

HUB CITY: ABERDEEN

Once known as the Port of Missing Men for its tendency to see male residents end up either murdered or awakened from a drunken stupor to find themselves unwillingly conscripted into service aboard a ship bound for Asia (a practice known as being "shanghaied"), Aberdeen today is very much a modern port city that plays a critical role in Washington's maritime infrastructure. Founded in 1911, the Port of Grays Harbor is Washington's only deepwater port on the Pacific Ocean, hosting ninety-six deepwater ships and barges in 2020. It is the leading commercial seafood landing port in Washington and moves over 3.2 million metric tons of cargo into and out of the state annually.

Aberdeen was founded in 1884 and named after a local salmon cannery honoring the city in Scotland, which is also located at the confluence of two rivers. Along with its working-class upbringing came a bevy of brothels, saloons and gambling establishments. However, those types of businesses are often an inevitability in a town experiencing a good deal of success in industry. For decades, Aberdeen's shoreline was lined with sawmills, canneries, shipbuilding outfits and other maritime enterprises, until the Great Depression put most of them out of business. Aberdeen remains a predominantly blue-collar city to this day but has seen a resurgence in prosperity thanks to its growing tourism industry.

From Aberdeen, maritime explorers can either take Highway 109 along the north side of Grays Harbor to visit Ocean Shores, Moclips, Taholah and all points in between or take Highway 105 along the south side of the harbor to visit Westport, Grayland and several interesting destinations along the way. However, visitors shouldn't be tempted to breeze through Aberdeen without making a few maritime-related stops first. For example, at the southern end of Twenty-Eighth Street in neighboring Hoquiam (pronounced "HOH-kwee-um") is a public boat launch next to an observation tower that provides 360-degree views of Grays Harbor, the port property, the cities of Hoquiam and Aberdeen and the mouth of the Hoquiam River.

Grays Harbor Historical Seaport

No visit to Aberdeen's maritime attractions would be complete without a stop at the Grays Harbor Historical Seaport, home of the state's official tall ship, *Lady Washington.* For over twenty-five years, the seaport has been providing educational, vocational, recreational and ambassadorial activities and experiences that promote and preserve Washington's maritime history. A 501(c)3 nonprofit, the seaport helps educate thousands of students with one-of-a-kind educational field trips.

The Grays Harbor Historical Seaport is currently planning a massive construction project to create a twenty-three-acre mixed-use waterfront area that reflects the rich history and character of Grays Harbor and the Olympic Peninsula. Dubbed Seaport Landing, the soon-to-be-built development will provide community access to the waterfront and an accessible dock for *Lady Washington.* Supporters intend Seaport Landing to blend small businesses with arts, heritage, recreational and educational opportunities that will serve the entire region. When completed, Seaport Landing will feature an interpretive center, a hotel and restaurant, a waterfront trail and park, moorage for tall ships, a spar shop for producing ship masts and maritime wood products and more.

Seaport Landing is scheduled to open sometime in the coming years. However, the story of the *Lady Washington* began long before the idea of Seaport Landing was even conceived. The original ship took part in the American Revolutionary War after it was constructed in the 1750s and was named after Martha Washington, wife of George Washington. It is thought to be the first American vessel to sail around Cape Horn, at the southern tip of South America, in 1787, and the first to make landfall on the North American West Coast the following year. Captained by Robert Gray, the *Lady Washington*—along with the larger *Columbia Rediviva,* commanded by John

In a historic recreation, two Native Salish-design canoes and paddlers from the Chinook Tribe give permission for the reproduced eighteenth-century ship *Lady Washington* and its crew to visit the tribe's ancestral lands at the mouth of the Columbia River. *Lisa Elliott/ Chinook Tribe.*

Kendrick—arrived in what is now Washington in 1788 with the intention of collecting furs and selling them in China. Gray's and Kendrick's efforts helped open trade in the Pacific after the *Lady Washington* became the first American ship to visit the Hawaiian Islands, Hong Kong and Japan.

Two centuries later, as the state of Washington commemorated its centennial in 1989, the Grays Harbor Historical Seaport launched a full-size replica of the *Lady Washington* into the Wishkah River on March 7 of that year. Skilled shipwrights partnered with historians to build the modern brig, which has appeared in several movies and TV shows, including *Pirates of the Caribbean* and *Star Trek: Generations*. Its overall length is 112 feet with a draft of 11 feet and a beam of 22 feet. The *Lady Washington*'s mast stands at 89 feet—perhaps in commemoration of both the ship's and the state's birth year. Depending on its configuration, it can utilize anywhere from three to six miles of rigging, requiring a crew compliment of twelve sailors capable of giving up to forty-five passengers at a time one of the most memorable experiences of their lives.

Until Grays Harbor Historical Seaport completes Seaport Landing and the *Lady Washington* has a home port befitting its lofty status, visitors may just be able to catch a glimpse of the state's namesake vessel moored at 500 North Custer Street—that is, if it hasn't been called into service once again, providing education and entertainment as it sails Washington's waters toward points unknown.

OCEAN SHORES

Located on the northern tip of the entrance to Grays Harbor, Ocean Shores has some of the most beautiful, expansive beaches to be found in Washington. On a sunny summer weekend, the town's population can easily swell from a little more than six thousand full-time residents to tens of thousands of sightseers. From its sandy shores to its meandering canal system, Ocean Shores features a raft of maritime experiences for any visitor to enjoy. The numerous restaurants and pubs offer fresh seafood dishes, while the gift shopping provides tourists with nautical knickknacks, candy and ice cream, antiques, crafts, kites and access to any number of outdoor activities, including moped, bicycle and horse rentals. There are plenty of hotels and rental properties throughout the area, so finding lodging is rarely an issue.

Though Ocean Shores was officially incorporated as a town in 1970, the history of the area goes back centuries. The peninsula was originally inhabited by members of the Quinault, Quileute, Queets, Hoh, Chehalis, Chinook and Cowlitz tribes and nations who were accustomed to digging clams, fishing and trading in the area. Their first encounter with non-Indigenous peoples occurred when Robert Gray sailed into what he named Bullfinch Harbor. Later, when George Vancouver revisited the harbor, he renamed it after Gray. Originally "Gray's" Harbor, the U.S. Board on Geographic Names dropped the apostrophe to conform with federal guidelines.

One of the first settlers to call the area home was A.O. Damon in 1861. Damon purchased the land that today comprises the city of Ocean Shores, and the southernmost tip of the peninsula is appropriately named Damon Point. As the years passed and more settlers began building homes in the area, it soon became a regular stop for the mail and supply boats coming from nearby Hoquiam to the east. Damon built a southern pier and a northern pier for that purpose, which dramatically increased the convenience of living in the new community.

In the 1960s, the Damon family sold the property to a visionary development group based out of Seattle, which hoped it would become a Pacific Northwest playground for California's rich and famous. One of the prime attractions would be the twenty-three miles of man-made freshwater canals that developers created to provide more waterfront property for potential buyers. They also built a golf course, a marina, an airport and the network of roads necessary to access the individual property lots when the town opened for business. Ocean Shores has since become one of Washington's favorite seaside getaway destinations.

The Wreck of the SS *Catala*

The Union Steamship Company of British Columbia, Canada, launched the coastal passenger and cargo steamship *Catala* in 1925. The ship was built in Montrose, Scotland, and Union named it after Catala Island at the entrance of Esperanza Inlet on the west coast of Vancouver Island. Catala Island was named in honor of a Catholic missionary, Father Magin Catalá, a 1793 resident of Santa Cruz de Nuca, a Spanish colonial settlement and the first European colony in British Columbia. The ship could hold 267 passengers and 300 tons of cargo and had a top speed of 14 knots.

Catala spent the next thirty years steaming up and down the western Canadian coastline carrying freight and passengers, until Union sold it to new owners in British Columbia for use as a fish-buying ship. The career change didn't last long, however, and by 1962, the new owners found a way to take advantage of a once-in-a-lifetime opportunity taking place in Seattle. It was the Century 21 Exposition, also known as the Seattle World's Fair, held April through October of that year. Nearly ten million people attended the fair, which prompted *Catala*'s owners to convert the ship into a boatel. Once the fair ended and the crowds dispersed, *Catala* found a home in Ocean Shores, working again as a boatel. For three years, *Catala* helped visitors to Washington's marvelous coastline enjoy their stay in a fun and unique fashion, but all that ended abruptly in 1965.

On a cold, wet and blustery New Year's Day, a winter storm hit Washington and wreaked havoc along its coastline. Entire beaches changed their shape or disappeared completely as the pounding waves eroded the shore, creating new beaches by depositing that sand elsewhere. In the tumult of the storm, *Catala* broke free of its moorings at Ocean Shores and fell victim to the

The SS *Catala*, seen here in the 1930s, spent as much of its eighty-year lifespan above the water as it did beneath the sand in Ocean Shores, Washington. *Walter E. Frost.*

mercilessly undulating surf. *Catala* rolled violently from port to starboard and back again for hours until the waves finally drove it like a spear tip deep into the heart of Damon Point, sometimes called Protection Island, at the mouth of Grays Harbor.

Efforts to refloat *Catala* failed, and the wreck was left to decay at the beach on Damon Point. For more than twenty years, it was vandalized and pillaged, and in the late 1980s, a girl broke her back after falling through a rusted portion of the deck. Her family sued the state, which in turn ordered the wreck torn down to sand level and buried, left to memories and sand crabs for nearly twenty more years. However, much like the New Year's Day storm in 1965, subsequent storms began to remove and displace material from *Catala*'s sandy grave, and the ship became exposed a little at a time. In the late 1990s, a succession of winter storms exposed enough of *Catala*'s hull to make it an unofficial Ocean Shores tourist attraction once again.

Then, in 2006, something happened that drove the last nail into *Catala*'s proverbial coffin. The storied ship that had seen just as much time above ground as below was about to meet its final and most resolute end. A beachcomber exploring the wreckage poked a piece of driftwood into an opening in the hull and discovered a thick black sludge dripping from the end of the stick. The state Department of Ecology quickly cleaned up the oil from *Catala*, recycled the remaining hull and reshaped the beach. Nary a shred of evidence can be found to indicate there was ever a once-proud eighty-one-year-old passenger liner turned quirky restaurant and hotel buried in the sand at Damon Point.

Coastal Interpretive Center

Less than half a mile from the *Catala* cleanup site is the Coastal Interpretive Center in Ocean Shores. Since 1977, the Coastal Interpretive Center (in one form or another) has been entertaining and educating thousands of visitors from all over the world. Specializing in hands-on exhibits, guided adventures and educational programming, the Coastal Interpretive Center presents user-friendly experiences focused on teaching visitors about the cultural and natural heritage of Washington's shores. That heritage includes the wreck of the SS *Catala*. Visitors to the center can touch artifacts from the ship, such as the original galley doors, china dishes and a transom window, as well as view captain's logs, a telegraph key and numerous pictures, all of which are displayed both inside the center and outside, along its western wall. There is even a piece of *Catala*'s hull bearing the storied ship's name.

Beyond the preponderance of *Catala* memorabilia, the Coastal Interpretive Center boasts an immense collection of seashells, rocks and minerals related to ocean life on display. In addition, it features an impressive collection of artifacts and stories from the Quinault Nation. Known for using the western red cedar for canoes, houses, clothing and more, the Quinault Nation is composed of several tribes from around the area. Visitors to the Coastal Interpretive Center can see a diorama meant to show what a typical Quinault village may have looked like prior to European American arrival.

The property surrounding the building is crisscrossed with interpretive walks where hikers can find native plant and bird identification signage along with remnants of Ocean Shores' humble beginnings, including the original carved seahorse from the Ocean Shores Inn and more recovered pieces of the *Catala* and other shipwrecks. The center at 1033 SE Catala Avenue offers visitors the opportunity to remember the experience by making a purchase at Damon's Outpost, the historically named bookstore that features postcards, handmade bookmarks, artwork and crafts made by local artists, rock tumblers, magnifying glasses, authentically collected glass floats and more.

Museum of the North Beach

Fifteen miles north of Ocean Shores is the town of Moclips, one of a half-dozen seaside communities along Highway 109 with eclectic histories. Though occupied by Native Americans for generations, it was settled by non-Indigenous residents in 1862 and platted in 1902. Moclips—a Native word pronounced "MOW-clips," just like it's spelled—quickly became a getaway destination for those looking to improve their health. The fitness fad of the early twentieth century gave rise to the first Moclips Beach Hotel built by Dr. Edward Lycan, a two-story, 150-room beachside resort that burned to the ground just months after it was completed in 1905. Undeterred, Dr. Lycan doubled down on his losses and built an enormous 325-room hotel on the site of the old building, billing it as the biggest hotel on the American west coast.

Completed in 1907, the second Moclips Beach Hotel was three stories high and a block long, boasting two thousand feet of covered veranda and a "perfect" view of the Pacific just twelve feet from the hotel grounds. Moclips was a resort town for the health-conscious in Washington and no doubt served its purpose well—until a series of terrible storms between 1911 and 1914 destroyed most of it, including its stores, restaurants, theater, canneries, lumber mills and the entire Moclips Beach Hotel.

Visitors to the seaside community today can learn more about this storied history at the Museum of the North Beach at 4658 State Route 109. The free museum relates many of the stories of numerous communities up and down the coastline, such as Copalis, Oyehut, Carlisle, Taholah and more. For example, the North Beach area was home to at least four schools that scheduled classes around the clamming tides so children could assist with the shellfish harvest. Artifacts from the myriad shipwrecks that occurred over the centuries are on display as well, including a matchbook and a room key from the SS *Catala* prior to its time as an Ocean Shores boatel.

In fact, so numerous are the recorded shipwrecks in the area that entire books have been written to detail each incident. As many a sailor has learned, the underwater topography off Washington's coast often combines with unfortunate weather patterns to generate a swift current that drives ships northward. Should a ship awaiting a pilot to escort it safely suddenly be cut loose by severe winds, it very well could meet the same deadly fate as dozens of others over the years. There have been all manner of ships grounded along the North Beach and subsequently destroyed by the pounding of the relentless surf—but perhaps none as dramatically as the British bark *Ferndale*.

Martha White and the Wreck of the *Ferndale*

Just after the New Year in 1892, a time of year notorious for bad maritime weather, the 240-foot sailing vessel *Ferndale* was hauling a load of coal and coke from Newcastle, New South Wales, Australia, to Portland, Oregon, when it got caught in a heavy current trying to enter the Columbia River. In a deep fog, despite the ship having its anchors out, the gale-force winds blowing from the southwest drove it some sixty miles to the north and ran it hard into the sands near Copalis just after three o'clock in the morning. As the ship listed severely to one side, the waves began smashing over the deck and washing away anything that wasn't tied down. Some crewmen grabbed life vests, while others lashed themselves to the masts or the rigging. An unfortunate few were simply washed overboard and vanished beneath the pounding surf.

After four relentless hours, the first shades of daylight began illuminating the nearby beach, and neighbors along the coast spotted the ship in distress. They notified homesteaders Edward and Martha White, who quickly dressed and made their way down to the beach to help. While Edward headed north, searching for survivors, Martha waved a white flag from shore and fired a pistol to get the attention of any crewmen still aboard the *Ferndale*. Around the same time, three sailors still aboard—seeing the futility of their situation—decided to untie themselves and swim for shore. Exhausted and frozen, Erick Sundberg, Charles Carlson and Peter Patterson leaped into the icy breakers and prayed for a miracle.

Barely conscious, Sundberg found his miracle when the twenty-five-year-old Martha spotted him being tossed about like a rag doll in the surf. She waded in, removed his waterlogged life preserver and dragged him up the beach to her house. Returning a few minutes later, she found Carlson

This 1901 image of the *Ernest Reyer*, a three-masted bark, stranded in the surf at the mouth of the Quinault River must have looked eerily familiar to locals who witnessed the similar fates of the *Abercorn* in 1888 and the *Ferndale* in 1892. *PSMHS, 5663.*

unconscious in the sand and dragged him to safety, as well. As she ran back to the water's edge, Martha saw Patterson caught in the waves just offshore. Like a scene from an action movie, Martha tore away part of her soaked skirt and dove in to rescue him. By the time she was able to pull him from the water, they both had reached their physical limit and collapsed onto the beach. Edward gathered several neighbors to bring Patterson inside to recover, but twenty or so crewmen did not survive the ordeal. The bodies of five others washed ashore in the following days and were buried nearby.

Word began to spread of Martha's heroism, aided by testimony from the surviving sailors, and soon, newspapers across the country had picked up and reprinted the story. State and federal politicians representing the area quickly petitioned the Treasury Department's Life-Saving Service to bestow on Martha a Gold Lifesaving Medal, which she received that July. The citizens of Portland, Oregon (where the cargo was destined), also honored Martha's efforts with a gold medal along with a cash reward. Travelers exploring Washington's North Beach today still sometimes find chunks of coal from the *Ferndale* washed up after a storm. Those who don't can always visit the Museum of the North Beach to see for themselves.

Quinault Cultural Center
and Museum in Taholah

The largest tribal reservation in western Washington belongs to the Quinault Indian Nation—anglicized from kʷínayɬ—a federally recognized tribe made up of Quinault and Queets Indians—along with descendants of the Quileute, Hoh, Chehalis, Chinook and Cowlitz Tribes—who consider themselves to be the "Canoe People" or the "People of the Cedar Tree." The reservation's 325 square miles are home to just over 1,500 individuals and headquartered at Taholah, the site of the largest village at the mouth of the Quinault River.

For countless generations, Indigenous people in this area lived with their family groups in longhouses, hunting, fishing and interacting with neighboring tribes. Some interactions with early European explorers were amicable, resulting in favorable trading and an exchange of cultural goodwill. Other interactions were not as fortunate, but through the centuries, the Quinault Nation has fiercely exerted its independence and desire to control

Noted historical photographer Edward S. Curtis captured this image of two Quinault Indians in a canoe collecting fish from a net in 1916. *Edward S. Curtis Collection, Library of Congress.*

its future. Through successful economic ventures such as the Quinault Pride Seafood company and the Quinault Beach Resort and Casino, the people today are seizing their own destiny. Nowhere is that story better told than at the Quinault Cultural Center and Museum in Taholah.

Exhibits at the museum, located at 807 Fifth Avenue, include stone tools, carvings, expertly preserved basketry, artwork, canoes, historical documents, field notes, photographs and books. Admission is free, but the tribe requests advance notice of an intended visit, so be sure to call ahead. Of course, visitors looking for a more contemporary experience offered by the tribe can check out the Quinault Beach Resort and Casino near Ocean Shores, which offers a wide variety of entertainment, dining and recreational opportunities for travelers around the Olympic Peninsula.

International Mermaid Museum

One of the most atypical attractions within the Maritime Washington National Heritage Area can be found along Highway 105 between Aberdeen and Westport. Located just outside the community of Markham, east of the John's River State Wildlife Area, is the International Mermaid Museum. Part of an independent business campus featuring the Westport Winery Garden Resort, the Ocean's Daughter Distillery and the Sea Glass Grill, the property is owned and operated by an enterprising couple who share a love of the ocean and its gifts.

Kim and Blain Roberts—both divers and former boat captains—began the grassroots effort to create their dream after relocating from Hawaii, where they had operated that state's biggest dive shop. Employing a brilliant idea, the museum teaches visitors about ocean ecology through mermaid mythology and is filled with an eclectic mix of scientific information, mystical mermaid lore from around the world and pop culture mermaid-related memorabilia. The walls are replete with stories of mermaid sightings through the centuries, the ceilings are adorned with mannequins in mermaid costumes and the ambient lighting gives visitors the feeling that they are indeed swimming beneath the surface as they make their way through the exhibits.

Promoting a "seashore to sea floor" theme, the International Mermaid Museum is as much undersea educational experience as it is social media–worthy selfie spot. Many of the artifacts and exhibits are fun and whimsical, while some elicit more somber reflections from visitors. Take, for example, the heavy, rusted diving helmet that was once worn while recovering casualties from the World War II bombing of Pearl Harbor. It is the Robertses' belief that sharing these underwater experiences and mythology can help unite coastal communities the world over—and they may be on to something. Since it opened, the International Mermaid Museum has welcomed thousands of visitors from around the globe.

After visiting the museum, explorers are free to roam the grounds and meander through the exquisitely designed gardens featuring over eighty sculptures and creations from local artists. There is, of course, a gift shop offering bottles of wine and spirits as well as myriad mermaid merchandise and plenty of parking for RVs, boat trailers and buses.

WESTPORT MARITIME MUSEUM AND THE GRAYS HARBOR LIGHTHOUSE

Located across Grays Harbor from Ocean Shores, Westport offers maritime explorers a multitude of experiences to enhance their oceanic appreciation. With a much deeper history than its cross-harbor counterpart, Westport plays the working waterfront to Ocean Shores' intended playground for the privileged. Though Westport was incorporated in 1914, the area along the south shore of Grays Harbor was long inhabited by the Chehalis Tribe, until a devastating smallpox outbreak wiped out thousands of their people and they were forced to move further inland. By the 1850s, sawmills, salmon canneries, commercial fishing operations and shipping outfits dotted the shoreline.

With the influx of marine industry came a need to rescue and protect mariners in danger. The national Life-Saving Service, established in 1871, soon built a station at Westport that included the Grays Harbor Lighthouse, a 107-foot monolith with a first-order Fresnel lens capable of shining a light visible at 23 miles out to sea. The government built the lighthouse atop a 12-foot-thick slab of sandstone nestled into the dunes just a few hundred feet away from the high tide line, and the lamps blazed to life in 1898. They remained lit until being electrically automated in the 1960s and were finally supplanted in the 1990s by a more modern navigational beacon.

In 2004, the Coast Guard formally turned over stewardship of Washington's tallest lighthouse to the Westport South Beach Historical Society, which had

The Westport Maritime Museum is located in the historic 1939 Coast Guard building and features a full-size whale skeleton as well as an illuminated first-order Fresnel lens from the Destruction Island Lighthouse. *Dan Nevill.*

been conducting tours of the century-old structure for many years. Aside from the creative architecture and technologically advanced features (for the time), one of the interesting things about the Grays Harbor Lighthouse today is that it stands on the same spot on which it was first built—but is now almost three thousand feet from the crashing waves. As the decades passed, the currents removed and redeposited sand from areas along Washington's coastline, slowly eroding beaches farther away and building new beachfront along Westport's western edge. In fact, maritime explorers brave enough to ascend the 135 steps of the iron spiral staircase will find the once-uninterrupted view of the Pacific mostly blocked now by scrubby pines that have grown up in the new soil.

Visits to the lighthouse at 1020 West Ocean Avenue can be arranged at the nearby Westport Maritime Museum. The museum at 2201 Westhaven Drive is housed in a 1939 Coast Guard station building designed to emulate traditional Nantucket architecture. It is one of five buildings within Westport's Marina District and showcases exhibits on the area's maritime history, the Coast Guard, a multitude of area shipwrecks, rescue operations and the whaling and fishing industries, as well as cranberry harvesting and logging. There is a plethora of marine environment artifacts and exhibits, including two outdoor exhibits featuring skeletons of sea mammals, a scale model of the former Coast Guard station, a knot-tying display and interpretive panels on beach erosion, ocean currents and marine mammals.

One of the museum's most stunning attractions is the first-order Fresnel lens relocated from the Destruction Island Lighthouse farther up the coast. Built in France in 1888 by Henry Lepaute from the design by Augustin-Jean Fresnel, the enormous arrangement of crystal prisms was first shipped by boat to the island and installed in 1891. After the Coast Guard removed it in 1995, it was transferred to Westport, where it has been mesmerizing visitors with a spectacular rotating light display ever since.

When finished visiting the Westport Maritime Museum, travelers are encouraged to stroll the waterfront along the marina and visit the various shops and vendors. Though still a working town where salty fishermen and women can be found boarding their commercial vessels daily in the dark and misty morning hours, Westport has also embraced its tourism side, offering visitors a number of seafood restaurant choices, candy and gift shops and charter excursions for fishing or whale watching. The jetty provides photographers with an endless supply of kaleidoscopic wave crashes, and the elevated viewing tower gives travelers a gull's-eye view of Half Moon Bay, Westhaven Cove and the entrance to Grays Harbor. There's even a small aquarium built in 1955 that continues to make sea life from Washington's marine waters accessible to the public.

PART V

COLUMBIA
RIVER

Pacific, Wahkiakum,
Cowlitz and Clark Counties

HUB CITY: RAYMOND

Seven miles south of Westport, explorers will find Pacific County, the southernmost part of the state still touching the ocean. The area was home to the Chinook and Chehalis Tribes for generations before diseases brought by European explorers, traders and fur trappers soon wiped out most of the Native population. By the time treaties were proposed in the mid-1800s, many of the area's Indigenous peoples had moved north to the Quinault Reservation and relinquished their traditional lands.

Given that the mighty Columbia River empties into the Pacific in this part of Washington, it's no surprise that the area has seen a succession of well-known maritime explorers. The mouth of the river was first mapped by Bruno de Heceta while sailing for Spain during his 1775 search for Russian settlements along the coast. In 1788, the British trader John Mears met with Indians in the area and renamed several of Heceta's landmarks. George Vancouver noted the river's entrance when he sailed past in early 1792, and Robert Gray finally traversed the treacherous bar and ventured upriver several months later. Lewis and Clark's Corps of Discovery expedition reached the end of its cross-country overland journey at what is now Pacific County in 1805.

The first half of the nineteenth century saw the area dominated by British and American fur trappers who harvested the virgin lands and sold their take at John Jacob Astor's trading post across the river in what would become Astoria, but the second half brought an influx of settlers to Pacific County by land and by sea. Many of those migrating families built lumber and shingle mills and began to harvest the area's plentiful natural resources through logging, fishing and manufacturing. One of the first places to find industrial success was Raymond, located at the confluence of the north and south forks of the Willapa River.

Raymond's name comes from one of the town's early homesteading families. Because of the city's location, early town leaders decided to build Raymond's business section and part of the residential section on stilts five or six feet above the tidelands and sloughs that crisscrossed the site. Elevated sidewalks and streets connected most of the buildings, and twice a day, the tides would wash away refuse under and around the town. By 1913, Raymond claimed a population of six thousand and had a reputation as a wild and woolly mill town. Community leaders fought the unwanted recognition with promotions of Raymond as "the Empire City of Willapa Harbor," "the City That Does Things" and "the City of Smokestacks." Thankfully, the smokestacks are gone today, and tidal action no longer plays a role in the city's cleanliness.

Willapa Seaport Museum

Before departing Raymond, maritime enthusiasts cannot miss stopping at the Willapa Seaport Museum at 310 Alder Street. Run by "Captain" Pete Darah, sometimes known as "Pirate Pete," the museum is filled floor to ceiling with information and insight into the area's history, including local shipbuilding, marine artifacts, naval battles, Indigenous peoples, lighthouses and much more. It is a must-see for anyone interested in the eclectic history of the region, but it's Pete's storytelling that puts the wind in the sails of the whole experience.

One story Pete recounts has a particularly cheerless ending. Some seventeen miles to the northwest of Raymond once stood the Shoalwater Bay Lighthouse and Life Saving Station. Proposed in 1857 and built in 1858, the lighthouse became a necessity after settlements further inland began growing thanks to oyster-harvesting and lumber activities. Atop its forty-two-foot tower, a fourth-order Fresnel lens was supposed to shine far out to sea but was evidently only visible for eleven miles even in the best of conditions—and nearly invisible in the worst. That, combined with the difficulty of getting food and supplies to the lighthouse keepers, caused the U.S. Lighthouse Board to close the Shoalwater Bay Lighthouse within a year.

The Willapa Seaport Museum in Raymond, Washington, is packed floor to ceiling with maritime and nautical artifacts. Its exhibits chronicle the various eras of the marine history of Washington State and beyond. *Washington Our Home*.

It reopened in 1861, however, and continued providing guidance to ships at sea as they rounded North Cove headed into Shoalwater Bay—but before the decade was out, it became clear that the small bluff on which the lighthouse stood was being threatened by coastal erosion. Nevertheless, the U.S. Life-Saving Service built a station at North Cove next to the lighthouse in 1877. The service doubled down on its investment in 1886 by building a new keeper's quarters, but the evidence pointing to the eventual washout of the land beneath the lighthouse and the station was irrefutable. The sea, it seemed, would not be stopped.

Shoalwater Bay, a name bestowed by English fur trader John Mears in 1788, became known as Willapa Bay in the 1890s. Around that same time, lighthouse and life-saving station keepers were feverishly erecting fences, planting shrubs and laying out brush mats in a fruitless attempt to prevent the land from being slowly washed away. For the next several decades, keepers fought in vain to protect their charges, but the relentlessness of the wind and waves simply could not be overcome.

A series of storms in the late 1930s left the lighthouse building with its foundation exposed and hanging precariously over the edge of the rapidly receding bluff. The U.S. Coast Guard assumed ownership of the station in 1939 and quickly removed any remaining records and equipment. The timing could not have been more expedient. A December storm in 1940 brought with it eighty-five-mile-per-hour winds, and the last remnants of the bluff supporting the lighthouse gave way, causing the entire structure to topple spectacularly over the bank and into the surf below.

The erosion didn't stop there, and the life-saving station—built some distance inland from the lighthouse—was soon in danger of meeting the same fate. The North Cove site finally closed in 1957, and remnants of this part of coastal history can be found throughout the Willapa Seaport Museum in Raymond. Admission is free, and with a little luck, Pirate Pete may just be on hand to give you a personal tour.

The Shoalwater Bay Tribe

Between Raymond and the North Cove lies the Shoalwater Indian Reservation, bifurcated by Highway 105 and consisting of about 350 acres plus a large area of tidelands. After many of the area's Indigenous peoples joined the Quinaults on their treaty-established reservation to the north in the 1850s, the remaining Lower Chehalis, Shoalwater Bay and Willapa Chinookan peoples banded together to continue living on their traditional lands. President Andrew Johnson formally set aside land for them by executive order in 1866, forming today's Shoalwater Bay Tribe.

Known as the "People of the Enclosed Bay," the Indians who make up the Shoalwater Bay Tribe once lived throughout the vast network of waterways from Ilwaco to Aberdeen. They made their living by fishing, hunting, catching crab and harvesting oysters, often selling part of their harvest to nearby canneries for income. The federally recognized tribe remains a sovereign nation, led by an elected five-member council and governed by a constitution. The people still tell their children stories from their ancestors and hold ceremonies the same way as their parents and grandparents did.

Today's Shoalwater Bay Tribe is strong and growing, working to ensure its children have a solid future ahead of them. From small and large business ventures to a multi-year plan to relocate the reservation to an area more protected from tsunamis, the tribe is finding success blending

The Indigenous peoples of Willapa Bay, known as Shoalwater Bay when Edward S. Curtis took this photo in 1913, incorporated as the Shoalwater Bay Tribe in 1866. *Edward S. Curtis Collection, Library of Congress.*

modern technologies and approaches with traditional heritage and culture. The tribal center at Tokeland serves as its headquarters, and visitors are encouraged to visit the tribe's casino and neighboring restaurants when passing through. Heritage explorers, however, may find the Shoalwater Bay Tribal Community Library and Museum at 4115 State Route 105 more interesting. Along with housing an extensive collection of Native American books, the library and museum help tell the story of the Shoalwater Bay Tribe by sharing its rich culture through art and historical artifacts.

THE OYSTER CAPITAL OF THE WORLD

Five miles to the southwest of Raymond is the city of South Bend, so named because it lies at the lowest point of a deep bend in the Willapa River. As travelers head along Highway 101 following the river as it leads to Willapa Bay, they'll pass by the Port of Willapa Harbor and the Raymond Port

Dock. Boaters who want to visit Raymond from the sea will find friendly moorage at the marina, which offers fuel, restrooms, a picnic area, service and maintenance facilities, a small store and other amenities. The entire area surrounding the mouth of the river is speckled with quaint farming communities, fishing villages, oyster farms, churches and pioneer cemeteries.

Throughout the short drive, the evidence of a century-old industrial era is visible. Eagle-eyed explorers will spot row upon row of ghost pilings that once supported the canneries, shipyards and mills built over the river itself. These scenes are interrupted occasionally by enormous white mounds that, on closer inspection, turn out to be oyster shells piled nearly two stories high. By the time visitors arrive in South Bend, it's clear why the small community bills itself as the Oyster Capital of the World.

In the middle of South Bend are two attractions that are sure to catch the attention of a maritime heritage enthusiast. The first, reminiscent of America's love affair with roadside oddities, is the "World's Largest Oyster"—and not the Guinness record–holding *Crassostrea gigas* measuring

Known as the "Oyster Capital of the World," South Bend, Washington, is one of the country's most plentiful locations for oysters, a claim reinforced by the giant concrete oyster shell sculpture located across from the Pacific County Museum. *Carol M. Highsmith, Library of Congress.*

nearly fourteen inches in length. It is, in actuality, a giant concrete sculpture of the top half of an oyster shell in Robert Bush Memorial Park. The statue makes for a great selfie stop when passing through South Bend. The park itself is named for a U.S. Navy hospital corpsman who was the youngest World War II veteran to receive the Medal of Honor for his heroic deeds. It also features several artistic sculptures, as well as an interpretive panel telling the story of a Chinook tribal legend of the portage lakes.

Directly across the street from the park is the Pacific County Historical Museum, an educational institution operated by the Pacific County Historical Society since 1970, where explorers can learn more about the area's industrial heritage, maritime history and more. Located at 1008 West Robert Bush Drive, the free museum's collection includes photos, records, artifacts and natural history objects that showcase Pacific County history.

Bay Center and the Chinook Indian Nation

Driving through the Niawiakum River Natural Area Preserve heading south on 101, travelers will pass a small outcropping of land called Goose Point, atop which is a small community named Bay Center. It's easy to miss as motorists race toward the well-promoted history and maritime beauty of Cape Disappointment at the mouth of the Columbia River. Bay Center, however, rightfully claims its own place in Washington history as the present headquarters of the Chinook Indian Nation.

The ancestral territory belonging to the five tribes of the Chinook Indian Nation stretches from Grayland, some twenty miles to the north, to Cannon Beach in Oregon, some fifty miles to the south, and east nearly to Longview. It is this vast area that welcomed Lewis and Clark in 1805 and about which so much was written in the papers and journals of the Corps of Discovery Expedition members as they neared the Pacific Ocean. The five tribes are the Clatsop, Kathlamet (or Cathlamet), Lower Chinuk (or Chinook), Waukikum (or Wahkiakum) and Weelappa (or Willapa).

Like that of so many other Indigenous peoples, the Chinookan way of life that included fishing, canoe carving, storytelling and hunting reached a turning point when they were asked to sign a treaty. At the Chehalis River Council in 1855, Isaac Stevens once again made promises to the area's Indigenous people in exchange for the relinquishing of their traditional lands. Days earlier, the Chinook had agreed to part with most

James G. Swan's 1857 image *Salmon Fishing at Chenook* illustrates how Chinookan people harvested salmon with nets, clubs, canoes and other fishing equipment along the north bank of the Columbia River. *Cowlitz County Historical Museum.*

of their territory in exchange for being allowed to remain where they were; however, Stevens's treaty made it clear they would be forced to relocate to the Quinault Reservation one hundred miles north. To the Chinookan people, the Quinaults were not friendly, and the five tribes understood that cohabitation would mean their eventual destruction. The Indians gathered at the council would not sign the treaty as Stevens had drafted it, and the governor concluded the interaction without succeeding.

Since then, the closest the Chinook Nation has come to a formal agreement with the U.S. government is when it briefly received federal recognition in 2001—for a fleeting eighteen months, after which it was rescinded without warning or convincing explanation. The exuberance that had rippled throughout tribal culture in western Washington and Oregon turned instantly to confusion, disbelief and anger. The culmination of hope for generations had been crushed with the stroke of a bureaucrat's pen.

For over twenty years, the Chinook Indian Nation has been fighting to regain its federal status, holding community meetings and public demonstrations, engaging in letter-writing campaigns and encouraging supporters to contact local, state and federal lawmakers to demand justice. Without formal recognition, the tribe cannot access resources such as housing, health care, utilities, food and more—even though their lands were taken from them without a treaty.

Many members of the Chinook Tribe live in Bay Center and in South Bend, both sites of ancient Indian villages. The tribe's ancestors lived in plank houses like the longhouses of other coastal tribes, made of old-growth western red cedar. Once the hub of Chinook life, plank houses were places to live, learn, worship, heal and escape from the harsh winter weather. Approximately eighty miles southeast of Bay Center, in the Ridgefield National Wildlife Refuge, is a full-size replica of a Chinookan plank house. While not directly maritime related, it is well worth a stop and a short hike when traveling down Interstate 5 between Kalama and Vancouver, especially for those interested in learning more about the Indigenous people of Washington.

HUB CITY: ILWACO

The city of Ilwaco (pronounced "ill-WAH-ko") is named after Elowahka Jim, the son-in-law of revered Chinookan chief Comcomly, the man who interacted with both Lewis and Clark as well as Robert Gray some sixty-seven years later. Initially called Unity in celebration of the country's reunification after the Civil War, when the town was platted in 1876, it was renamed Ilwaco. Located at the mouth of the Columbia River and the south end of the Long Beach Peninsula, Ilwaco was a critical juncture for both maritime and overland travelers.

Not much has changed about Ilwaco's geographic benefits in the past century and a half, and it remains a popular hub for explorers looking for recreational opportunities such as wildlife viewing, beachcombing, charter fishing and heritage tourism. One of the more interesting stories from the region is the development of the "Clamshell Railroad," which ran from Ilwaco north to Nahcotta between 1888 and 1930. The narrow-gage, independently operated rail line replaced the stagecoach for mail, passenger and cargo deliveries. Officially named the Ilwaco Railroad and Navigation Company (IR&N), the railroad followed the coastline up and down Long Beach so closely that its schedule was tide-dependent—leading one newspaper journalist facing a delay to dub it the "Irregular, Rambling and Never-Get-There Railroad."

Despite the cynical moniker, the Clamshell Railroad was mostly appreciated by residents of the peninsula who needed to get to Ilwaco to do their shopping, go to school or conduct other business. As with most of the country's small railroad lines, however, it was the automobile that rendered the railroad irrelevant. Though the tracks are long gone and most of the rail cars have been sold off, there are still a few places on Long Beach that can claim to have been one of the original stops on the Clamshell Railroad.

Columbia Pacific Heritage Museum

The best place to learn more about the IR&N, the character of Ilwaco and the people and events that comprise the area's history is the Columbia Pacific Heritage Museum, located at 115 SE Lake Street. In fact, the museum has restored one of the Clamshell Railroad's original passenger cars. Located outside the museum is the coach *Nahcotta*, built in 1889 by the Pullman Palace Car Company out of Chicago. It took the better part of thirty years to restore the last remnant of that bygone era, and to keep it in good condition, the museum allows visitors inside the car only a few times each year.

The museum also features exhibits on the Chinook people, as well as fishing, oyster harvesting, logging, tourism and lifesaving—a necessity for people living on a beach nearly thirty miles long. One of the most captivating tales told at the museum comes from the Klipsan Beach Life Saving Station, a storied structure that not only still stands today but has also been restored and can be rented out for unforgettably unique vacation experiences. Officially established in 1891, the station had been staffed for the previous two years by volunteers looking to prevent further catastrophes along Washington's southern coast. The area was known even then as the Graveyard of the Pacific on account of the number of ships that had run aground over the decades.

The Klipsan Beach Life Saving Station sits on a two-acre site that once belonged to Edwin G. Loomis, president of the Ilwaco Railroad and Navigation Company. Lifesaving crews could use the nearby railroad to move quickly to wrecks north and south of the station. Rescues were most often conducted using surfboats that crews kept stored on four-wheeled wagons in the boathouse. When called into action, the boats could be pulled down to the water's edge by horses, and the men could row out to the stranded ship to rescue the passengers before the ship broke apart in the surf. In later years, rescuers employed a special cannon that could shoot a rope out across the waves and, hopefully, onto the struggling vessel so sailors could be pulled to safety.

What was once the 1891 Ilwaco Beach Life Saving Station, now Klipsan Beach—integral to saving countless lives from dozens of shipwrecks—is now available for vacation rentals on the Long Beach Peninsula. *David Rush.*

In 1915, when the U.S. Life-Saving Service and the U.S. Revenue Cutter Services merged to become the U.S. Coast Guard, the station became known only as No. 309. After seven years, it was permanently closed, used briefly as a radio beacon during World War II and abandoned in 1947. The property was returned to the Loomis family, who soon sold it to other parties. Owners had the station house listed on the National Register of Historic Places in 1979, and it has since been restored and converted into three vacation rentals, which can accommodate a total of sixteen guests. This premier vacation spot for families is located at 22409 Pacific Way in Ocean Park, about ten miles north of the Columbia Pacific Heritage Museum.

CAPE DISAPPOINTMENT

One of the primary places a maritime explorer should visit in Washington, the area now known as Cape Disappointment State Park is replete with maritime history and heritage. Cape Disappointment guards the north side of the entrance to the Columbia River—dubbed Rio de San Roque when it was first mapped in 1775. The cape itself was named by British captain John Mears in 1788 after he failed to locate the entrance to the river, and Robert Gray is credited with being the first to sail a ship across the treacherous bar and into the river itself. To mark the momentous achievement, Gray renamed the river Columbia after the ship he was commanding, the *Columbia Rediviva*.

In 1805, Lewis and Clark's expedition arrived near Cape Disappointment toward the end of its eighteen-month, 3,700-mile journey from St. Louis, Missouri. While the rest of the Corps of Discovery sheltered upriver at a place called Dismal Nitch, Lewis continued to the cape and questioned local Chinook Indians about their dealings with other non-Indigenous people in the area. Within a few decades, the waters around the cape became so busy with ships that the U.S. Lighthouse Board authorized construction of a lighthouse atop the highest bluff overlooking the mouth of the river. After ten shipwrecks in 1852 and 1853, the area was given the name Graveyard of the Pacific, a dubious distinction that has since spread to cover an area from Canada's Vancouver Island to Tillamook Bay in Oregon. To date, it has claimed more than two thousand unfortunate marine vessels and over one thousand lives.

Cape Disappointment Lighthouse opened in 1856, making it the oldest operating lighthouse in the state. Adventurers today can make the short hike out to the lighthouse while skirting around a beautifully secluded rocky beach called Deadman's Cove. The entire area is filled with photo opportunities, especially once hikers reach the lighthouse itself, and the view of the Columbia emptying into the Pacific is nothing short of overwhelming. However, ships heading south along the coast once complained of difficulty spotting the lighthouse, so a second one at North Head on the Pacific side of Cape Disappointment opened in 1898. This lighthouse is maintained by a nonprofit that also operates an impressive gift shop in the carriage barn. It's directly across from the keeper's quarters, which can also be rented out for vacation stays.

During the Civil War, there were concerns that enemies would attempt to infiltrate the area via the Columbia River, so the United States positioned several cannons at Cape Disappointment in 1862. The installation was named Fort Canby in 1875, and much like those of other coastal fortifications in Washington, Fort Canby's bunkers and artillery mounts are still in place, waiting to be explored. There are interpretive panels scattered around the site to educate visitors about the fort, but parents with young children should

After the Cape Disappointment Lighthouse became operational in 1856, mariners approaching the Columbia River from the north complained they could not see the light until they had nearly reached the river. Thus, the North Head Lighthouse was built in 1898. *Brian Morris.*

be aware of high ledges and rusted metal doors, many of which have sharp, weathered edges despite frequent new coats of paint.

Cape Disappointment is also home to the largest U.S. Coast Guard search and rescue station on the Northwest coast and the oldest in the district, first established as a Life-Saving Service station in 1877. The station also hosts the Coast Guard's National Motor Lifeboat School, which makes use of nine vessels, including a fifty-two-foot motor lifeboat, two forty-seven-foot motor lifeboats and two twenty-nine-foot response boats. Station "Cape D," as it's known, provides search and rescue to commercial and recreational mariners within fifty nautical miles of the Columbia River entrance, responding to hundreds of calls for assistance every year. Though maritime technology has advanced, and long jetties built on either side of the river in the early twentieth century have mitigated some of the danger, weather conditions rarely change much over time. During winter storms, ocean swells often reach as high as thirty feet and combine with strong outgoing tides and currents, leading to predictably unpredictable seafaring conditions across the bar even today.

Lewis and Clark Interpretive Center

One of the most distinguishing attractions to be found at Cape Disappointment is the Lewis and Clark Interpretive Center, located just a stone's throw from the Fort Canby bunkers at 244 Robert Gray Drive. Easily one of the most comprehensive institutions in Washington dedicated to telling the story of the early American explorers, the center stands high atop cliffs overlooking both the Pacific Ocean and the Columbia River.

Once immersed in the museum, guests will come face to face with actual artifacts from the famous expedition, including a handmade wooden razor box thought to have been carved by Sacagawea herself. The Lewis and Clark Interpretive Center presents the entire ordeal, with a thoughtful and complete interpretation of every aspect of the journey, and the top floor of the museum is dedicated to local maritime and military history. A plaque just outside belies the importance of the location, proclaiming, "Welcome to the edge of the continent." Thankfully, the edge of the continent has a well-stocked gift shop.

However, if a cost-free Lewis and Clark experience is desired, adventurers can travel seven miles upstream (twelve if driving east on 101) to Middle Village, also known as Station Camp. Chinook Indians had spent countless seasons at their central dwelling place by the time the Lewis and Clark expedition made it their last camp in Washington. The Chinook had migrated to their winter village at the time, so the American explorers found the area unoccupied. Naming it Station Camp, they spent just ten days there—but its foothold in American history was secured when Lewis made day trips from there to lay eyes on the Pacific for the first time.

Two and a half miles upriver is Dismal Nitch, a place where—over 217 years ago—the Corps of Discovery expedition was pinned down by wind and rain for six days. It's now a Department of Transportation rest area with a covered billboard detailing different aspects of the journey. A few paces west of the rest area lies a monument that commemorates the importance of the stopover. It's a beautifully made bronze relief sculpture depicting the party attempting to soldier on through the sleet and is absolutely worth a stop just to admire the artist's work.

KNAPPTON COVE HERITAGE CENTER

Twenty miles east of the hub city of Ilwaco, maritime explorers will find one of the most unique interpretive sites in Washington. The Knappton Cove Heritage Center at 521 State Route 401 is a small, unassuming building with a wooden sign reading "U.S. Quarantine Station, 1899–1938" that should cause any traveler to pause long enough to wonder about the history of such a place. Indulging in that curiosity, in this case, will be well rewarded, given that it once bore the nickname "the Ellis Island of the Pacific."

The Knappton Cove Heritage Center, formerly the historic Columbia River quarantine station, was one of many hospitals and health facilities operated by the U.S. Public Health Service during the country's foundational period. In its first year of operation, staff inspected 6,120 immigrants and crewmen passing through the Columbia River. By the time it closed in 1938, approximately 100,000 immigrants and crew had been inspected at the quarantine station. The waters in front of the property today reveal hundreds of foundational pilings at low tide—remnants of the past that leave a footprint of what once was considered a shield for the Columbia River.

Between 1899 and 1938, immigrant ships coming through the Columbia River would quarantine at Knappton Cove until free of diseases such as bubonic plague, yellow fever, cholera, smallpox and typhus. *Knappton Cove Heritage Center.*

An American homesteader first claimed ownership of the land from the Chinook people, and in 1876, the land was sold to the Eureka & Epicure Packing Company, a cannery that employed dozens of Chinese workers. As maritime businesses increasingly sprang up along the Columbia, immigrants began flooding into the area from overseas. Concerns about communicable diseases grew, and the federal government purchased the cannery in 1898 to convert it into a quarantine station. For nearly forty years, European and Asian immigrants suffering from the bubonic plague, yellow fever, cholera, smallpox, typhus and other maladies passed through health inspection at this facility.

Those who weren't granted clearance would often be isolated until their symptoms improved, and staff at the quarantine station would frequently have to fumigate entire ships and delouse passengers' personal items. These tactics, antiquated as they may seem, proved effective in preventing an epidemic in the Pacific Northwest. By 1938, however, medical advances and better health controls led to the closing of the quarantine station, which was later sold off and converted into a recreational fishing camp in the 1950s.

Housed in one of the station's original buildings, the Knappton Cove Heritage Center tells stories that are both inspiring and heartbreaking, macabre yet cathartic, and provide visitors with a fascinating glimpse into life before modern medicine and sanitary standards. Admission is free, and donations are greatly appreciated.

HUB CITY: LONGVIEW

During World War I, Kansas City timber magnate Robert Alexander Long realized he was running out of resources to keep his company going. He started scouting new locations from California to British Columbia and found Kelso, which was located at the confluence of the Cowlitz and Columbia Rivers. Long didn't want another squalid, sprawling mill town to develop at his new site, so he created what was then the largest planned city ever built entirely with private funds, sited it next to Kelso and called it Longview.

Long's community grew into a major industrial force during the mid-twentieth century, and the Port of Longview is now one of the busiest in the state. Featuring eight marine terminals and 835 acres of waterfront industrial property, the port plays a vital role in the local economy by providing manufacturing as well as maritime jobs. Originally built to export the lumber and paper products developed by the Long-Bell Lumber Company, the Port of Longview today moves all types of cargos and commodities such as fertilizers, grain, lumber and logs, minerals, paper, steel and more.

The vast amount of riverfront in Longview allows for industrial as well as commercial and recreational use. Though Longview is located over fifty miles from the Pacific Ocean, tidal action still influences life in the waterfront community. There are numerous parks, public boat launches, fishing piers and local swimming holes located in the area, and nearly all of them have a connection to local history. The best place to learn more about Longview, Kelso and other communities in the area is at the Cowlitz County Historical

Museum, located at 405 Allen Street. Its mission is to celebrate the evolving cultural heritage of the people of the Lower Columbia region, honoring the community's past through dynamic, informative interpretations and personal stories from its history.

THE COWLITZ TRIBE

Prior to the creation of Longview, the area was home to the Cowlitz Indian Tribe (anglicized from káwlicq). Known as "the Forever People," their heritage comes from at least two major groups: the Upper Cowlitz people, who occupied a huge area northeast of where Longview is today, and the Lower Cowlitz people, who lived in villages along the Cowlitz River. When the tribe gained federal recognition in 2000, the two groups were united and given a reservation in Ridgefield, though they are headquartered in Longview.

Cowlitz Tribe member Robert Harju carved this "shovel nose" canoe in 2015, which is representative of the type of canoes Cowlitz people used on rivers in the 1800s. *Cowlitz County Historical Museum.*

The Cowlitz people had frequent interactions with non-Indigenous fur trappers and traders in the early to mid-nineteenth century, but unlike their coastal neighbors, the Cowlitz relied more on hunting and harvesting than annual salmon runs for food. They instead fished for smelt, a small, oily fish that closely resembles trout and migrates through inland rivers in considerable numbers. To catch smelt, the Cowlitz would use dugout canoes that had a different shape than those found on the ocean. Where coastal canoes were designed with high, pointed prows meant for cutting through waves, inland canoes had long, flat bows on which a fisherman could stand in calm waters.

Today's Cowlitz Tribe is as dedicated to preserving its heritage as it is to ensuring a solid future. The tribe has developed modern health clinics and housing units and are continuing to expand their newest venture, ilani, located on the Cowlitz Reservation in Ridgefield. ilani is a gaming, shopping, dining and meeting destination, featuring eighteen different restaurants, bars and retail outlets. For explorers looking for more contemporary recreation among the Cowlitz people, ilani would be an excellent choice. However, if history and traditional culture are a preferred experience, the free Cowlitz County Historical Museum offers several exhibits dedicated to the tribe and its heritage. There's a hands-on basket creation station where visitors can learn about weaving, as well as interpretive panels, artifacts, murals and photographs that tell stories of Indigenous culture and a gift shop offering books about the Cowlitz people and their way of life.

Stella's Cigar Rafts

Small-town residents around Washington are usually proud of their history. One of the most devoted communities in Washington can be found nestled along the banks of the Columbia River about ten miles west of Longview on Highway 4. The area now known as Stella is mentioned in the journals of Lewis and Clark, who passed the rugged bluffs toward the end of their long journey to the Pacific. Facing the blistering winds and relentless rain for which western Washington is known, the Corps of Discovery explorers took what little refuge they could at the base of those cliffs. And following them came waves of pioneers looking to settle the American West.

Stella was once a bustling hive of timber, commerce and riverboat activity, and as it grew between the river and vast forested areas, Stella became an

Loggers and boatmen created ocean-going "cigar rafts," so named for their shape, in Stella, Washington. The lumber would be towed by tugboats down the Columbia River and out to the Pacific Ocean, bound for places like San Francisco, California. *Washington State Archives.*

integral part of Washington's timber industry. Lumbermen would cut trees and drag them down the hillsides to be processed in Stella, which had sawmills right on the river's shore. Then, logs were floated together downriver, out onto the Pacific and on to their various destinations. However, fierce ocean storms would sometimes break the log booms apart, sending logs crashing back onto nearby beaches. Inventive mill workers then began constructing a new type of boom that was more secure and easier to transport by ship and contained more logs than traditional booms.

These booms were called cigar rafts because when bound together, they looked like giant cigars. After the first logs were chained into a sturdy frame, new logs could be added to the structure vertically, taking up less surface area on the water. After loading the logs, workers would secure the ends with heavy chains, and the cigar raft was ready to be towed downriver by tugboats. Trees processed in Stella helped build Fisherman's Wharf in San Francisco along with dozens of other facilities up and down the West Coast.

Many of the people who today call Stella home have ancestors who helped build those log rafts, and they're keeping the memories of their loved ones alive. Explorers who stop in Stella can visit the Stella Historical Society Museum at 8530 Ocean Beach Highway to gain an appreciation of the effort and dedication that helped build the town. Though the cigar rafts are long gone, one look through the museum will reveal remnants of the past sure to entertain and educate visitors of all ages.

Transportation Interpretive Center

About ten miles south of Longview on Interstate 5 is Kalama (pronounced "kuh-LAMB-uh"), a smaller city with an active port on the Columbia River and a collection of unique history. Kalama was the seat of Cowlitz County from 1872 to 1922, before Longview took that title. The town was first settled by non-Indigenous people in 1853, and its name is thought to be a Cowlitz Indian word or possibly the name of a Hawaiian man who settled in the Pacific Northwest sometime in the 1830s. In 1870, the Northern Pacific Railway chose Kalama as the terminus of its new line from Duluth, Minnesota; however, by the time workers laid the tracks north to Tacoma, the company decided to make that city on Puget Sound its terminus instead of Kalama on the Columbia.

Though Kalama lost its impending prominence, the Northern Pacific still had railroad tracks from its new terminus to Kalama, and the company decided to continue the railroad line south—albeit across the river in Oregon. What that meant for transportation is that a ferry was needed that could transport an entire train across the river between the two communities in a single trip. That's how the side-wheel steamer *Tacoma* secured its place in local maritime history. Between 1884 and 1908, whenever trains would roll into town, track workers would use a switching locomotive to separate the cars, load them onto three rail sets affixed to *Tacoma*'s 360-foot deck, then paddle across the river to offload and reassemble the train on the other side.

After its last run, the *Tacoma* was sold and stripped; its new owners removed the engines and made a barge out of the hull. On a foggy night many years later, as it was being towed through Puget Sound near its namesake city, it was struck broadside by another ship and sank to the bottom, where it has remained ever since. It's a sad ending for a once-useful and unique Pacific Northwest maritime vessel, but divers today continue to use the site for training. Underwater video of the wreckage shows the rails still affixed to the deck of *Tacoma*'s hull.

To move railroad cars across the Columbia River from Kalama, Washington, to Goble, Oregon, the Northern Pacific Railroad used a specially designed sidewheel ferry, the *Tacoma*, between 1884 and 1908. *Kalama Public Library*.

This story and myriad more are interpreted for the public at the Port of Kalama's Transportation Interpretive Center, a critical stop for any maritime traveler exploring the Columbia River region. Exhibits within treat visitors to immersive displays, models (including an intricate replica of the *Tacoma*), videos, artifacts and vehicles such as a dugout cedar canoe from the Cowlitz Tribe.

The Transportation Interpretive Center at 110 West Marine Drive is located between McMenamins Kalama Harbor Lodge—a boutique hotel and restaurant inspired by the Hawaiian heritage of John Kalama— and the recently renovated Port of Kalama Marina—which includes permanent slips for up to 222 vessels and over seven hundred feet of public guest dock space.

As a bonus, an eight-minute walk south along the waterfront from the lodge will lead guests to the Ahles Point Cabin, a waterfront bistro also operated by McMenamins. Its name is a clever adaptation (McMenamins is also a brewery, after all) of the area known as Ahle Point, where steamboats would often stop to pick up passengers and cargo along the Columbia

River. Visitors to this soft, sandy beach today just may find themselves in the right place at the right time, as the American Cruise Line company still uses Ahle Point as a stopover when it brings up to 180 passengers to Kalama aboard its authentic sternwheel paddleboat. Watching the huge historical replica ship glide easily onto the shores of Ahle Point and drop its gangplank may be best experienced with a McMenamins brew in one hand and a camera in the other.

HUB CITY: VANCOUVER

Vancouver is located about one hundred miles upriver from the mouth of the Columbia, and its shores still rise and fall with the Pacific Ocean tides. Originally established around 1825, Vancouver was officially incorporated in 1857. It is the oldest non-Indian settlement in the state, and with its age comes a bevy of historically important events.

The area was long occupied by the Chinook Tribe; when Lewis and Clark spent nine days there, they proclaimed it to be the best site for settlement west of the Rockies. Twenty years after their historic journey, the Hudson's Bay Company established a fur-trading post and named it Fort Vancouver after their countryman who had explored the Pacific shores in the late 1700s. After the area became United States territory in 1846, the U.S. Army established what was then the largest military installation on the West Coast at Vancouver, which is also home to Pearson Field, the oldest airfield still operating in the West.

Vancouver today is considered a suburb of the larger city of Portland, Oregon. It has the third-oldest port in the state, situated on two thousand acres west of where Interstate 5 crosses the Columbia. The Port of Vancouver oversees five million metric tons of cargo annually, including steel, wheat, automobiles, wind turbines, pulp and more. East of the port, the city has invested in developing its downtown waterfront area. Explorers can choose from half a dozen restaurants and, on balmy evenings, eat on the nearby Grant Street Pier. After-dinner options include a stroll along the Waterfront Renaissance Trail, exploring a few accessible beaches or walking the Discovery Historic Loop trail, featuring several history-related sculptures.

Fort Vancouver National Historic Site

One of Vancouver's most popular attractions for history buffs is the Fort Vancouver National Historic Site, a replica of the Hudson's Bay Company (HBC) trading post for which the city is named. When looking for a new location to site HBC's Pacific headquarters in 1824, the company's chief factor scouted terrain all the way from the mouth of the Columbia until he selected the area that is now Vancouver. The area's gently sloping plains, fertile soil and location on the north side of the river all contributed to the decision. At the time, the British believed that the boundary between United States and British territory would be drawn at the river, so choosing a southern shore location could have been potentially disastrous.

Over the next two decades, Fort Vancouver was the primary location for all maritime trade traffic. The HBC's power and wealth grew in tandem with the increasing number of ships that sailed one hundred miles up the Columbia to do business at the fort. However, the Treaty of Oregon in 1846

The British Hudson's Bay Company's Fort Vancouver, parts of which have been restored as a historic site in Vancouver, Washington, was once the center of social, economic and political activity in the Pacific Northwest, as seen in this 1840s lithograph. *Public domain.*

established the border not along the Columbia River but the forty-ninth parallel, much farther north. Realizing they were now on U.S. land, the chief factor relocated the fort's supplies and personnel to Victoria along the Strait of Juan de Fuca and turned over ownership of the property to the U.S. Army. Today's Fort Vancouver has been meticulously recreated to look as it would have at the height of its prominence.

There are numerous other sights worth seeing around Fort Vancouver, but one of particular interest to maritime heritage enthusiasts stands just outside the Fort Vancouver visitor center and gift shop at 1501 East Evergreen Boulevard. A few paces from the entrance is a stone slab with the faces of three men carved on it, each half of its base depicting one half of a boat. One side of the slab is etched with Japanese writing, while the other is embedded with a plaque describing how three Japanese sailors lost their way in a storm in 1832. Their cargo ship disabled, the crew drifted for fourteen months at sea before running aground on what is now the Washington coast near Cape Flattery. Captured by the Makah Indians, the three men lived with the tribe for a brief time before the Makahs brought them south to Fort Vancouver to turn them over to the Hudson's Bay Company. These three men—Iwakichi, Otokichi and Kyukichi—became the first known Japanese to set foot on the North American continent.

Henry J. Kaiser Memorial Shipyards

Located a short drive south of the Fort Vancouver area is an industrial waterfront that would ordinarily not attract even the least bit of attention. Visitors looking in the right place, however, will find something remarkable that is arguably underappreciated in Vancouver's maritime history. South of Highway 14 (the Lewis and Clark Highway), at the end of SE Marine Park Way, is the Henry J. Kaiser Memorial Shipyards observation tower. The three-story triangular platform is adorned with numerous interpretive panels telling the story of how one man and an unshakable labor force helped the United States win World War II.

In 1942, Kaiser came to Vancouver and obtained two hundred acres of riverfront land to build a shipyard that supplied America with ships for the war effort in the Pacific. Between then and 1946, the Kaiser Shipyard was the nation's most versatile, churning out 141 vessels of 5 different types—nearly 1 a week during its operation. Included in the final tally were 10 liberty ships,

The workers at Kaiser Shipyards in Vancouver, Washington, built sixteen Liberty ships, thirty-one Victory ships, fifty escort carriers, twenty-one troop transport ships and thirty LST landing ships during World War II. *U.S. Navy Photo.*

30 tank-landing ships, 50 escort aircraft carriers (known as "baby flattops," they could carry and launch 37 planes each), 31 troop transports and 8 cargo ships, among others. These ships launched from one of 12 bays that released vessels to the waiting river on rail lines.

Running these shipyards were tens of thousands of men and women who served as welders, shipwrights, painters, riveters, shipfitters, machinists, electricians, crane operators and more. They had come by invitation from Kaiser himself, who recruited across the country with promises of good pay, housing and medical care. The biggest crowd Vancouver had ever seen in one place gathered on April 5, 1943, when Eleanor Roosevelt christened one of the shipyard's latest creations. Eyewitnesses estimate around seventy-five thousand workers, residents and guests turned out to greet the first lady as she smashed a bottle of champagne across the bow of the USS *Alazon Bay*.

Exploring the area today, visitors might have a challenging time spotting the shipways through the trees that have grown over the years. Study the photographs in the panels affixed to the tower, then look harder at the industrial site across the public boat launch, and you can see through the undergrowth the outlines of concrete walls and ramps disappearing into the river. While the sight of aircraft carriers lined up on the Vancouver waterfront may never be witnessed again, there are still remnants of that monumental effort visible to explorers who look in just the right places today.

Adventurers who want to know more about the Kaiser Shipyards, the steamships that once darted back and forth across the river or the Native peoples and pioneers who have called the area home throughout the years can visit the Clark County Historical Museum at 1511 Main Street in Vancouver. The museum's permanent and rotating exhibits continue to interpret the history of the area for visitors in interactive and entertaining ways.

Captain William Clark Park at Cottonwood Beach

Seventeen miles east of Vancouver on the Lewis and Clark Highway is the town of Washougal (pronounced "wah-SHOO-gull"), which is an anglicization of the Chinookan word Washuxwal, meaning "rushing water." It is the farthest place upriver on the Columbia where tidal action is measurable. It is also a place where the Chinookan people have existed for at least the last four thousand years, according to archaeological evidence found in the area. The "rushing water" refers to where Washington's Washougal River and Oregon's Sandy River empty into the Columbia across from each other.

On their return trip home in 1806, the Corps of Discovery needed to stock up on foodstuffs, as the spring salmon had not yet returned and local Indians told them food was scarce upriver. This worried the party, so for nearly a week, they made camp approximately where today's Captain William Clark Park is at Cottonwood Beach. The explorers spent the time hunting along both sides of the river until the men had killed elk, bear and deer, dried the meat at the campsite and packed it into their canoes. With fresh game in their stores, the explorers ventured confidently forth to make the upriver journey back to St. Louis.

Visiting the park today, adventurers will find replicas of those canoes lining Cottonwood Beach. Let children climb in for a great picture and a learning opportunity to educate them about not only the successful voyage of Lewis and Clark but also the Indigenous people who came to their aid in their time

On March 31, 1806, the Lewis and Clark Corps of Discovery expedition made camp along the Columbia River while securing provisions for the long return journey home to St. Louis, Missouri. Today, their preparation is memorialized by several canoe sculptures along the waterfront at Cottonwood Beach in Washougal, Washington. *Rene Carroll*.

of greatest need. After spending time at the park, travelers should make their way into town to visit the Two Rivers Heritage Museum at 1 Durgan Street in Washougal. Not only is it replete with artifacts and photos from the town's early years, but it also features exhibits on the Corps of Discovery expedition as well as the Indigenous people who have lived in the area for generations.

SELECTED BIBLIOGRAPHY

Articles

Kresge, Joanna. "What Are Those Ships on Ruston Way's Waterfront?" *South Sound Magazine*, January 28, 2016; updated October 4, 2022. https://www.southsoundmag.com/arts-entertainment/what-are-those-ships-on-ruston-way-s-waterfront/article_114aa84a-a693-5b0d-aefb-b205d05baf47.html.

Lile, Stephanie. "The Curious Case of the *La Merced*." Harbor Mystery Museum, updated March 20, 2020. https://www.harbormysterymuseum.org/post/the-curious-case-of-the-la-merced.

Shaw, Katie. "Hansville Home Is Like a Ship Out of Water." *Kitsap Daily News*, August 21, 2014.

Books

Fowler, Chuck, and Mark Freeman. *Tugboats on Puget Sound*. Charleston, SC: Arcadia Publishing, 2009.

Fowler, Chuck, and the Puget Sound Maritime Historical Society. *Tall Ships on Puget Sound*. Charleston, SC: Arcadia Publishing, 2007.

Hitchman, James H. *A Maritime History of the Pacific Coast of America 1540–1980*. Landham, MD: University Press of America, 1990.

Newell, Gordon, ed. *The H.W. McCurdy Marine History of the Pacific Northwest, 1895–1965*. Seattle, WA: Superior Publishing, 1966.

———. *The H.W. McCurdy Marine History of the Pacific Northwest, 1966–1975*. Seattle, WA: Superior Publishing, 1977.

Wright, E.W., ed. *Lewis & Dreyden Marine History of the Pacific Northwest*. New York: Antiquarian Press, 1961. First published 1895 by Lewis & Dreyden (New York).

Websites

Black Ball Ferry Line: https://cohoferry.com

Chinook Indian Nation: https://chinooknation.org

Commissioned Corps of the U.S. Public Health Service: https://www.usphs.gov

Cowlitz Indian Tribe: https://cowlitz.org

Duwamish Tribe: https://www.duwamishtribe.org

Historic Naval Ships Association: https://www.hnsa.org

HistoryLink: https://historylink.org

Hoh Tribe: https://hohtribe-nsn.org

Jamestown S'Klallam Tribe: https://jamestowntribe.org

Lewis and Clark Trail Heritage Foundation: http://lewisandclark.org

Lighthouse Friends: https://lighthousefriends.com

Lower Elwha Klallam Tribe: https://www.elwha.org

Lummi Nation: lummi-nsn.gov

Makah Tribe: https://makah.com

Nisqually Tribe: http://www.nisqually-nsn.gov

Port Gamble S'Klallam Tribe: https://www.pgst.nsn.us

Puget Sound Maritime Historical Society: https://pugetmaritime.org

Puget Sound Naval Shipyard: https://www.navsea.navy.mil

The Puyallup Tribe of Indians: http://puyallup-tribe.com

Quileute Nation: https://quileutenation.org

Quinault Indian Nation: http://quinaultindiannation.com

Samish Indian Nation: https://samishtribe.nsn.us

Shoalwater Bay Tribe: https://shoalwaterbay-nsn.gov

Skokomish Indian Tribe: https://skokomish.org

South Sound Maritime Heritage Association: https://www.maritimeoly.org

Squaxin Island Tribe: https://squaxinisland.org

Steilacoom Tribe: https://www.steilacoomtribe.com

Suquamish Tribe: https://suquamish.nsn.us

Swinomish Indian Tribal Community: https://swinomish-nsn.gov

Tulalip Tribes: https://www.tulaliptribes-nsn.gov

United States Coast Guard: https://www.uscg.mil

U.S. Life-Saving Service Heritage Association: https://uslife-savingservice.org

Washington Department of Archaeology and Historic Preservation: https://dahp.wa.gov

Washington State Archives: https://www.sos.wa.gov/archives/

Washington State Department of Transportation: https://wsdot.wa.gov

Washington State Parks: https://parks.wa.gov

Washington Trust for Historic Preservation: https://preservewa.org

PHOTO ATTRIBUTIONS

Page 87: *Maiden of Deception Pass* (cropped). Sean O'Neill, Creative Commons Attribution NoDerivs 2.0 Generic, https://creativecommons.org/licenses/by-nd/2.0.

Page 119: *Andrew and Bertha Skansie Net Shed House* (cropped). Sreasons7, Creative Commons Attribution 4.0 International, https://creativecommons.org/licenses/by-sa/4.0.

Page 122: *Steilacoom Tribal Cultural Center* (perspective). Joe Mabel, Creative Commons Attribution ShareAlike 3.0 Unported, https://creativecommons.org/licenses/by-sa/3.0.

Page 129: *Yelm Jim's fish trap at Puyallup Indian reservation, circa 1885*. State Library Photograph Collection, 1851–1990, Washington State Archives, Digital Archives, http://www.digitalarchives.wa.gov.

Page 161: *Makah Petroglyphs in Olympic Peninsula National Park*, Aliaksei Baturytski, Shutterstock.com.

Page 164: *OCNMS Ruby Beach Overlook* (cropped). Nick Zachar/NOAA, Creative Commons Attribution 2.0 Generic, https://creativecommons.org/licenses/by/2.0

Page 171: *S.S. "Catala,"* Walter E. Frost, City of Vancouver Archives (Canada), Item CVA 447-2080.

Page 179: *Westport Maritime Museum* (cropped). Dan Nevill, Creative Commons Attribution 2.0 Generic, https://creativecommons.org/licenses/by/2.0.

Page 203: *Cigar Style Piling Raft Ready to Leave Down River for Astoria Then to San Francisco.* John T. Labbe Collection of Logging and Railroad Photographs, 1892–2010, Washington State Archives, Digital Archives, http://www.digitalarchives.wa.gov.

Insert, page 7, top: *Tacoma, WA—Fireboat No. 1—03* (cropped). Joe Mabel, Creative Commons Attribution ShareAlike 3.0 Unported, https://creativecommons.org/licenses/by-sa/3.0.

Insert, page 11, top: *Point Roberts, Lighthouse Marine Park*—view of the lighthouse and shore with blue ocean in the background. Klara Steffkova, Shutterstock.com.

Insert, page 15, bottom: *Fishing Boat Maritime Museum Flag Westport Grays Harbor Puget Sound Washington State Pacific Northwest.* Bill Perry, Shutterstock. com.

ABOUT THE AUTHORS

Erich R. Ebel was born in Spokane, Washington, and has had stories to tell ever since. He received a bachelor's degree in communications from Washington State University, spent ten years as a TV and radio journalist and has spent the past eighteen years in government and nonprofit communications and marketing. When Erich decided to pursue his passion—the history, heritage and culture of Washington, the greatest state in the lower forty-eight—he created a communications and marketing consulting company that caters to small museums and historical societies, among other clients.

Erich has lived on the green side of Washington as well as the brown side. He's navigated its rivers and climbed its mountains. He's fished its lakes, hiked its trails, marveled at its geology and studied its fascinating, storied history. Erich's blog, videos and podcasts hold a treasure trove of interesting facts, unknown facets and fascinating tales that help educate the public about the amazing and unique experience of being in Washington. Learn more at www.WashingtonOurHome.com.

rowing up in Tacoma on Puget Sound, Chuck Fowler has had a lifelong interest in maritime history, ships and sea stories. He is author of three Washington state maritime history books and numerous published articles. Chuck is past president of the Puget Sound Maritime Historical Society in Seattle and a former trustee of the Washington State Historical Society and State History Museum. In 2013, he received the Robert Gray Medal for distinguished leadership in state and local history, the society's highest honor. A retired marketing and communications consultant, he specialized in maritime heritage, waterfront revitalization and tourism development projects.

Chuck holds a bachelor's degree from the University of Puget Sound and master's degree from Northwestern University. For ten years he was volunteer co-coordinator of the Pacific Northwest Maritime Heritage Council, and he is past president of the South Sound Maritime Heritage Association in Olympia. Chuck served on the planning and steering committees that led, in 2019, to the establishment of the Maritime Washington National Heritage Area, a program of the National Park Service.